Weather and Climate Inventory
National Park Service
Northeast Coastal and Barrier Network

Natural Resource Technical Report NPS/NCBN/NRTR—2006/008
WRCC Report 06-07

Christopher A. Davey, Kelly T. Redmond, and David B. Simeral
Western Regional Climate Center
Desert Research Institute
2215 Raggio Parkway
Reno, Nevada 89512-1095

September 2006

U.S. Department of the Interior
National Park Service
Natural Resource Program Center
Fort Collins, Colorado

The Natural Resource Publication series addresses natural resource topics that are of interest and applicability to a broad readership in the National Park Service and to others in the management of natural resources, including the scientific community, the public, and the National Park Service conservation and environmental constituencies. Manuscripts are peer-reviewed to ensure that the information is scientifically credible, technically accurate, appropriately written for the intended audience, and designed and published in a professional manner.

The Natural Resource Technical Reports series is used to disseminate the peer-reviewed results of scientific studies in the physical, biological, and social sciences for both the advancement of science and the achievement of the National Park Service's mission. The reports provide contributors with a forum for displaying comprehensive data that are often deleted from journals because of page limitations. Current examples of such reports include the results of research that addresses natural resource management issues; natural resource inventory and monitoring activities; resource assessment reports; scientific literature reviews; and peer reviewed proceedings of technical workshops, conferences, or symposia.

Views and conclusions in this report are those of the authors and do not necessarily reflect policies of the National Park Service. Mention of trade names or commercial products does not constitute endorsement or recommendation for use by the National Park Service.

Printed copies of reports in these series may be produced in a limited quantity and they are only available as long as the supply lasts. This report is also available from the Natural Resource Publications Management website (http://www.nature.nps.gov/publications/NRPM) on the Internet or by sending a request to the address on the back cover.

Please cite this publication as follows:

Davey, C. A., K. T. Redmond, and D. B. Simeral. 2006. Weather and Climate Inventory, National Park Service, Northeast Coastal and Barrier Network. Natural Resource Technical Report NPS/NCBN/NRTR—2006/008. National Park Service, Fort Collins, Colorado.

NPS/NCBN/NRTR—2006/008, September 2006

Table of Contents

Table of Contents (continued)

Figures

Tables

Appendixes

Acronyms

AASC	American Association of State Climatologists
ACIS	Applied Climate Information System
AFB	Air Force Base
ASIS	Assateague Island National Seashore
ASOS	Automated Surface Observing System
AWOS	Automated Weather Observing System
BLM	Bureau of Land Management
CACO	Cape Cod National Seashore
CASTNet	Clean Air Status and Trends Network
COLO	Colonial National Historical Park
COOP	Cooperative Observer Program
CRN	Climate Reference Network
CWOP	Citizen Weather Observer Program
DFIR	Double-Fence Intercomparison Reference
DST	daylight savings time
EPA	Environmental Protection Agency
FAA	Federal Aviation Administration
FIIS	Fire Island National Seashore
FIPS	Federal Information Processing Standards
GATE	Gateway National Recreation Area
GEWA	George Washington Birthplace National Monument
GMT	Greenwich Mean Time
GOES	Geostationary Operational Environmental Satellite
GPMP	Gaseous Pollutant Monitoring Program
GPS	Global Positioning System
GPS-MET	NOAA ground-based GPS meteorology
I&M	NPS Inventory and Monitoring Program
LEO	Low Earth Orbit
LST	local standard time
NADP	National Atmospheric Deposition Program
NCDC	National Climatic Data Center
NCBN	Northeast Coastal and Barrier Inventory and Monitoring Network
NERCC	Northeast Regional Climate Center
NetCDF	Network Common Data Form
NOAA	National Oceanic and Atmospheric Administration
NPS	National Park Service
NRCS	Natural Resources Conservation Service
NWS	National Weather Service
POMS	Portable Ozone Monitoring System
PRISM	Parameter Regression on Independent Slopes Model
RAWS	Remote Automated Weather Station Network
RCC	regional climate center
SAHI	Sagamore Hill National Historic Site
SAO	Surface Airways Observations Network

Surfrad	Surface Radiation Budget Network
SNOTEL	Snowfall Telemetry Network
THST	Thomas Stone National Historic Site
USDA	U.S. Department of Agriculture
USGS	U.S. Geological Survey
UTC	Coordinated Universal Time
WBAN	Weather Bureau Army Navy
WMO	World Meteorological Organization
WRCC	Western Regional Climate Center
WX4U	Weather For You Network

Executive Summary

Climate is a dominant factor driving the physical and ecologic processes affecting the Northeast Coastal and Barrier Inventory and Monitoring Network (NCBN). Climate variations are responsible for short- and long-term changes in ecosystem fluxes of energy and matter and have profound effects on underlying geomorphic and biogeochemical processes. The NCBN parks contain critical coastal and wetland habitat for rare and endangered species. These areas also act as important migratory corridors for various animal species. Imposed on these characteristics is a long history of human uses in the NCBN region. The natural systems of the NCBN are being stressed by ongoing population growth in the northeastern U.S., which is occurring particularly in coastal areas. Because of its influence on the ecology of NCBN park units and the surrounding areas, climate was identified as a high-priority, vital sign for the NCBN, and climate is one of the 12 basic inventories to be completed for all National Park Service (NPS) Inventory and Monitoring Program (I&M) networks.

This project was initiated to inventory past and present climate monitoring efforts in the NCBN. In this report, we provide the following information:

- Overview of broad-scale climatic factors and zones important to NCBN park units.
- Inventory of weather and climate station locations in and near NCBN park units relevant to the NPS I&M Program.
- Results of an inventory of metadata on each weather station, including affiliations for weather-monitoring networks, types of measurements recorded at these stations, and information about the actual measurements (length of record, etc.).
- Initial evaluation of the adequacy of coverage for existing weather stations and recommendations for improvements in monitoring weather and climate.

Temperatures in the NCBN generally decrease from south to north and are moderated significantly compared to adjacent inland locations due to the proximity of the Atlantic Ocean. Despite this moderating influence of the Atlantic Ocean, January minimum temperatures are generally under -5°C in the northern park units of the NCBN. Summers in the region are warm and humid, with July mean maximum temperatures ranging between 22-30°C for NCBN park units. Mean annual precipitation for NCBN park units generally ranges from 1000 to 1200 mm. Precipitation is more common during the summer months for the southern park units of the NCBN, while precipitation is more common during the winter months in the northern park units. Tropical cyclones and nor'easters are both extreme storm events that occasionally introduce large-scale disturbances into NCBN ecosystems. These disturbances have been noted with storms such as the "Perfect Storm" of October, 1991. Significant positive trends in temperature and precipitation have been reported over the region. Future climate changes in the eastern U.S. are expected to influence the intensity and frequency of ice storms, tropical cyclones, and other extreme storm events in the region.

Preliminary work has been accomplished by the NCBN office to identify weather/climate stations within NCBN park units, particularly those at Cape Cod National Seashore

(CACO). Through an accompanying search of national databases and inquiries to NPS staff, we have identified 20 weather/climate stations that are at or within NCBN park units. These include four stations with Assateague Island National Seashore (ASIS), eight stations with Cape Cod National Seashore (CACO), one station with Fire Island National Seashore (FIIS), and seven stations with Gateway National Recreational Area (GATE). Most of these stations are either National Weather Service (NWS) Cooperative Observer Program (COOP) stations or NWS/Federal Aviation Administration (FAA) Surface Observation Network (SAO) stations. There are no weather/climate stations located at or within Colonial National Historical Park (COLO), George Washington Birthplace National Monument (GEWA), Sagamore Hill National Historic Site (SAHI), and Thomas Stone National Historic Site (THST). These park units are small and therefore must rely heavily on stations outside of the park units for their weather and climate data.

Most of the park units in NCBN have a relatively dense coverage of weather and climate stations in or near park boundaries. This is true especially for the park units near New York City and on Long Island. However, GEWA and THST currently have very limited station coverage. There is only one reliable long-term record available within 30 km of GEWA. Despite its proximity to the Washington, D.C. metropolitan area, THST has only two reliable long-term climate records within 30 km of its boundaries. These records come from SAO stations. In light of this situation, the continued operation of those COOP and SAO stations with long-term climate records is critically important. Active partnerships between NPS and the NWS offices in this region can help ensure that these valuable stations remain active and provide useful data for NPS research and management activities.

At the present time, metadata records are severely lacking for many of the local NPS weather and climate stations that were identified by previous climate station inventories for the NCBN. We could not identify basic metadata such as station name, latitude and longitude, elevation, and station period of record for most of these stations. We therefore encourage continued efforts to collect such metadata for local NPS weather and climate stations.

Acknowledgements

This work was supported and completed under Task Agreement H8R07010001 with the Great Basin Cooperative Ecosystem Studies Unit. We would like to acknowledge helpful assistance from various National Park Service personnel associated with the Northeast Coastal and Barrier Inventory and Monitoring Network. Particular thanks are extended to Bryan Milstead, Sara Stevens, and Marc Albert. We also want to thank John Gross, Margaret Beer, Grant Kelly, Heather Angeloff, and Greg McCurdy for their assistance. Seth Gutman with the National Oceanic and Atmospheric Administration Earth Systems Research Laboratory provided valuable input on the GPS-MET station network. Portions of the work also were supported by the Western Regional Climate Center under the auspices of the National Oceanic and Atmospheric Administration.

1.0. Introduction

Weather and climate are key drivers in ecosystem structure and function. Global- and regional-scale climate variations will have a tremendous impact on natural systems (Chapin et al. 1996; Schlesinger 1997; Jacobson et al. 2000; Bonan 2002). These variations influence the fundamental properties of ecologic systems, such as soil–water relationships, plant–soil processes, and nutrient cycling, as well as disturbance rates and intensity. These properties, in turn, influence the life-history strategies supported by a climatic regime (Neilson 1987).

It is essential that park units within the Northeast Coastal and Barrier Inventory and Monitoring (I&M) Network (NCBN) have an effective climate-monitoring system in place to track climate changes and to aid in management decisions relating to these changes. Most park units observe weather and climate elements as part of their overall mission. The lands under NPS stewardship provide many excellent locations for monitoring climatic conditions. Although the vital signs monitoring plan for the NCBN (Stevens et al. 2005) does not mention any specific objectives for climate and weather monitoring in the NCBN, such monitoring efforts have been identified as being crucially important for the region (CACO 2001). Atmospheric processes are critical to mineral and nutrient cycling through NCBN ecosystems. Knowledge of trends in precipitation, storm frequency and intensity, deposition chemistry, and atmospheric ozone levels are essential to understanding and interpreting why changes in species composition, community structure, water and soil chemistry, or dynamic processes are occurring. More specifically, long-term climate monitoring is fundamental to the Long-term Coastal Ecosystem Monitoring Program at Cape Cod National Seashore (CACO 2001).

The purpose of this report is to determine the current status of weather and climate monitoring within the NCBN (Figure 1.1). Eight park units are represented in the NCBN (Table 1.1). In this report, we provide the following informational elements:

- Overview of broad-scale climatic factors and zones important to NCBN park units.
- Inventory of locations for all weather stations in and near NCBN park units that are relevant to the NPS I&M networks.
- Results of metadata inventory for each station, including weather-monitoring network affiliations, types of recorded measurements, and information about actual measurements (length of record, etc.).
- Initial evaluation of the adequacy of coverage for existing weather stations and recommendations for improvements in monitoring weather and climate.

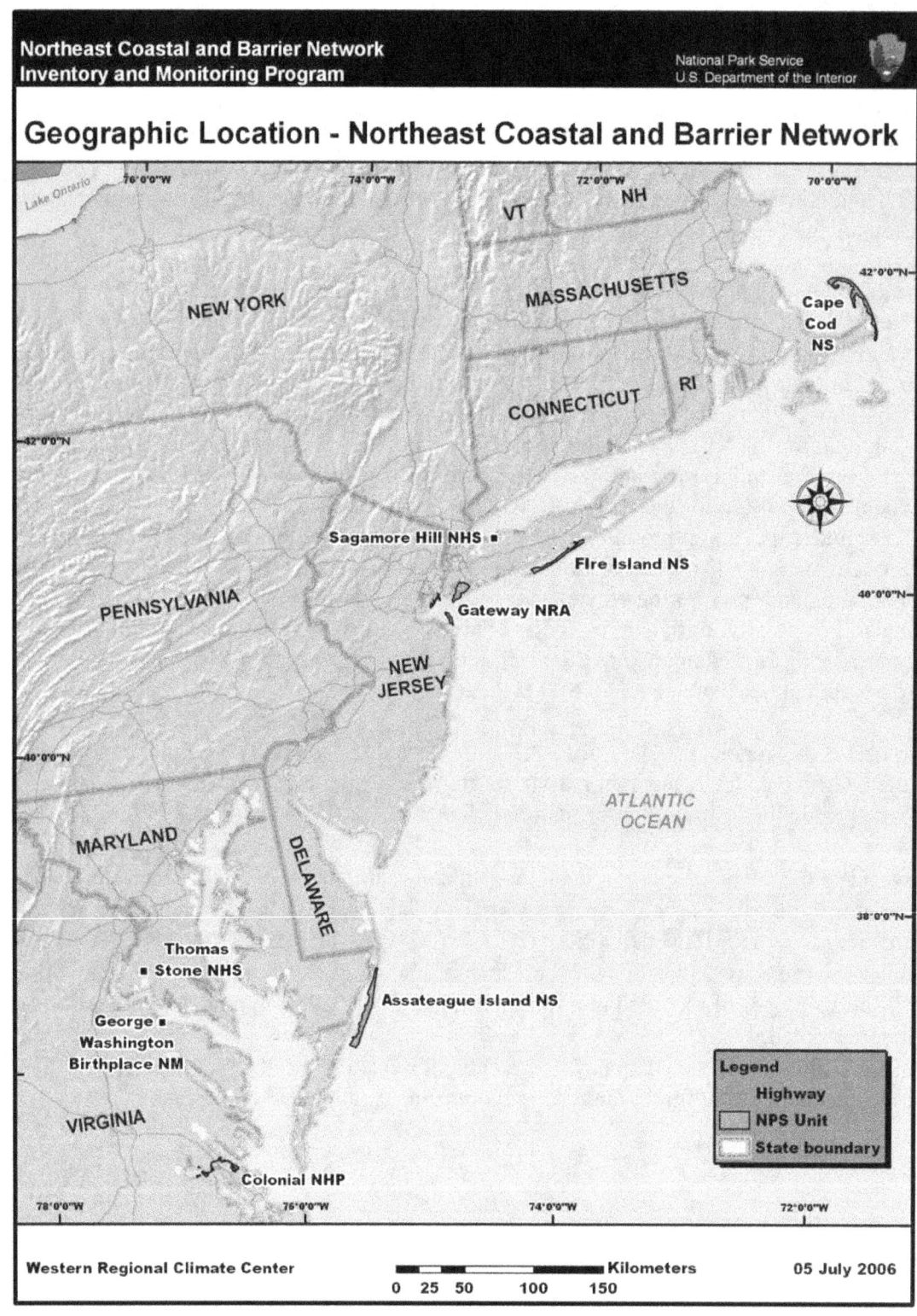

Figure 1.1. Map of the Northeast Coastal and Barrier Inventory and Monitoring Network.

Table 1.1. Park units in the NCBN.

Acronym	Name
ASIS	Assateague Island National Seashore
CACO	Cape Cod National Seashore
COLO	Colonial National Historical Park
FIIS	Fire Island National Seashore
GATE	Gateway National Recreation Area
GEWA	George Washington Birthplace National Monument
SAHI	Sagamore Hill National Historic Site
THST	Thomas Stone National Historic Site

1.1. Network Terminology

Before proceeding, it is important to stress that this report discusses the idea of "networks" in two different ways. Modifiers are used to distinguish between NPS I&M networks and weather/climate station networks. See Appendix A for a full definition of these terms.

1.1.1. Weather/Climate Station Networks

Most weather and climate measurements are made not from isolated stations but from stations that are part of a network operated in support of a particular mission. The limiting case is a network of one station, where measurements are made by an interested observer or group. Larger networks usually have more and better inventory data and station-tracking procedures. Some national weather/climate networks are associated with the National Oceanic and Atmospheric Administration (NOAA), including the National Weather Service (NWS) Cooperative Observer Program (COOP). Other national networks include the interagency Remote Automated Weather Station network (RAWS) and the NWS/Federal Aviation Administration (FAA) Surface Airways Observation Network (SAO). Usually a single agency, but sometimes a consortium of interested parties, will jointly support a particular weather/climate network.

1.1.2. NPS I&M Networks

Within the NPS, the system for monitoring various attributes in the participating park units (about 280–290 in total) is divided into 32 NPS I&M networks. These networks are collections of park units grouped together around a common theme, typically geographical.

1.2. Weather versus Climate Definitions

It is also important to distinguish whether the primary use of a given station is for weather purposes or for climate purposes. Weather station networks are intended for near-real-time usage, where the precise circumstances of a set of measurements are typically less important. In these cases, changes in exposure or other attributes over time are not as critical. Climate networks, however, are intended for long-term tracking of atmospheric conditions. Siting and exposure are critical factors for climate networks, and it is vitally important that the observational circumstances remain essentially unchanged over the duration of the station record. Some climate networks can be considered hybrids of weather/climate networks. These hybrid climate networks can supply information on a short-term "weather" time scale and a longer-term "climate" time scale.

In this report, "weather" generally refers to current (or near-real-time) atmospheric conditions, while "climate" is defined as the complete ensemble of statistical descriptors for temporal and spatial properties of atmospheric behavior (see Appendix A). Climate and weather phenomena shade gradually into each other and are ultimately inseparable.

1.3. Purpose of Measurements

Inventorying and monitoring climate activities should be based on a set of guiding fundamental principles. The starting point in evaluating weather/climate monitoring programs begins with asking the following question:

- What is the purpose of weather and climate measurements?

Evaluation of past, present, or planned weather/climate monitoring activities must be based on the answer to this question.

Weather and climate data and information constitute a prominent and widely requested component of the NPS I&M networks (I&M 2006). As primary environmental drivers for the other "vital signs," weather and climate patterns present various practical and management consequences and implications for the NPS (Oakley et al. 2003). Within the context of the NPS, the following services constitute the main purposes for recording weather and climate observations:

- Provide measurements for real-time operational needs and early warnings of potential hazards (landslides, mudflows, washouts, fallen trees, plowing activities, fire conditions, aircraft and watercraft conditions, road conditions, rescue conditions, fog, restoration and remediation activities, etc.).
- Provide visitor education and aid interpretation of expected and actual conditions for visitors while they are in the park and for deciding if and when to visit the park.
- Establish engineering and design criteria for structures, roads, culverts, etc., for human comfort, safety, and economic needs.
- Consistently monitor climate over the long-term to detect changes in environmental drivers affecting ecosystems, including both gradual and sudden events.
- Provide retrospective data to understand *a posteriori* changes in flora and fauna.
- Document for posterity the physical conditions in and near the park units, including mean, extreme, and variable measurements (in time and space) for all applications.

The last three items in the preceding list are pertinent primarily to the NPS I&M networks; however, all items are important to NPS operations and management. Most of the needs in this list overlap heavily. It is often impractical to operate separate climate measuring systems that

4

also cannot be used to meet ordinary weather needs, where there is greater emphasis on timeliness and reliability.

1.4. Design of Climate-Monitoring Programs

Determining the purposes for collecting measurements in a given weather/climate monitoring program will guide the process of identifying weather/climate stations suitable for the monitoring program. The context for making these decisions is provided in Chapter 2 where background on the NCBN climate is presented. However, this process is only one step in evaluating and designing a climate-monitoring program. This process includes the following additional steps:

- Define park and network-specific monitoring needs and objectives.
- Identify locations and data repositories of existing and historic stations.
- Acquire existing data when necessary or practical.
- Evaluate the quality of existing data.
- Evaluate the adequacy of coverage of existing stations.
- Develop a protocol for monitoring the weather and climate, including the following:
  - o Standardized summaries and reports of weather/climate data.
  - o Data management (quality assurance and quality control, archiving, data access, etc.).
- Develop and implement a plan for installing or modifying stations, as necessary.

Throughout the design process, there are various factors that require consideration in evaluating weather and climate measurements. Many of these factors have been summarized by Dr. Tom Karl, director of the NOAA National Climatic Data Center (NCDC), and widely distributed as the "Ten Principles for Climate Monitoring" (Karl et al. 1996a; NRC 2001). These principles are presented in Appendix B, and the guidelines are embodied in many of the comments made throughout this report. The most critical factors are presented here. In addition, an overview of requirements necessary to operate a climate network is provided in Appendix C, with further discussion in Appendix D.

1.4.1. Need for Consistency

A principal goal in climate monitoring is to detect and characterize slow and sudden changes in climate through time. This is of less concern for day-to-day weather changes, but it is of paramount importance for climate change. There are many ways whereby changes in techniques for making measurements, changes in instruments or their exposures, or seemingly innocuous changes in site characteristics can lead to apparent changes in climate. Safeguards must be in place to avoid these false sources of temporal "climate" variability if we are to draw correct inferences about climate behavior over time from archived measurements.

For climate monitoring, consistency through time is vital, counting at least as important as absolute accuracy. Sensors record only what is occurring at the sensor—this is all they can detect. It is the responsibility of station or station network managers to ensure that observations are representative of the spatial and temporal climate scales that we wish to record.

1.4.2. Metadata

Changes in instruments, site characteristics, and observing methodologies can lead to apparent changes in climate through time. It is therefore vital to document all factors that can bear on the interpretation of climate measurements and to update the information repeatedly through time. This information ("metadata," data about data) has its own history and set of quality-control issues that parallel those of the actual data. There is no single standard for the content of climate metadata, but a simple rule suffices:

- Observers should record all information that could be needed in the future to interpret observations correctly without benefit of the observers' personal recollections.

Such documentation includes notes, drawings, site forms, and photos, which can be of inestimable value if taken in the correct manner. That stated, it is not always clear to the metadata provider *what is important* for posterity and *what will be important* in the future. It is almost impossible to "over-document" a station. Station documentation is underappreciated greatly and seldom thorough enough (especially for climate purposes). Insufficient attention to this issue often lowers the present and especially future value of otherwise useful data.

The convention followed throughout climatology is to refer to metadata as information about the measurement process, station circumstances, and data. The term "data" is reserved solely for the actual weather and climate records obtained from sensors.

1.4.3. Maintenance

Inattention to maintenance is the greatest source of failure in weather/climate stations and networks. Problems begin to occur as soon as sites are deployed. A regular visit schedule must be implemented, where sites, settings (e.g., vegetation), sensors, communications, and data flow are checked routinely (once or twice a year at a minimum) and updated as necessary. Parts must be changed out for periodic recalibration or replacement. With adequate maintenance, the entire instrument suite should be replaced or completely refurbished about once every five to seven years.

Simple preventative maintenance is effective but requires much planning and skilled technical staff. Changes in technology and products require retraining and continual re-education. Travel, logistics, scheduling, and seasonal access restrictions can consume major amounts of time and budget but are absolutely necessary. Without such attention, data gradually become less credible and then often are misused or not used at all.

1.4.4. Automated versus Manual Stations

Historic stations often have depended on manual observations and many continue to operate in this mode. Manual observations frequently produce excellent data sets. Sensors and data are simple and intuitive, well tested, and relatively cheap. Manual stations have much to offer in certain circumstances and can be a source of both primary and backup data. However, methodical consistency for manual measurements is a constant challenge, especially with a

6

mobile work force. Operating manual stations takes time and needs to be done on a regular schedule, though sometimes the routine is welcome.

Nearly all newer stations are automated. Automated stations provide better time resolution, increased (though imperfect) reliability, greater capacity for data storage, and improved accessibility to large amounts of data. The purchase cost for automated stations is higher than for manual stations. A common expectation and serious misconception is that an automated station can be deployed and left to operate on its own. In reality, automation does not eliminate the need for people but rather changes the type of person that is needed. Skilled technical personnel are needed and must be readily available to operate automated stations, especially if real-time communications are in place and data gaps are not wanted. Site visits are needed at least annually and spare parts must be maintained. Typical annual costs for sensors and maintenance are $1.5–2.5K per station per year.

1.4.5. Communications

With manual stations, the observer is responsible for recording and transmitting station data. Data from automated stations, however, can be transmitted quickly for access by research and operations personnel, which is a highly preferable situation. A comparison of communication systems for automated and manual stations shows that automated stations generally require additional equipment, more power, higher transmission costs, attention to sources of disruption or garbling, and backup procedures (e.g. manual downloads from data loggers).

Automated stations are capable of functioning normally without communication and retaining many months of data. At such sites, however, alerts about station problems are not possible. As a result, station failures can often go undetected for considerable amounts of time, allowing large data gaps to develop. Two-way communications between the station and the host server for the station permit recovery in full from such disruptions, along with increased capabilities to reprogram data loggers remotely and better opportunities for diagnostics and troubleshooting. In virtually all cases, two-way communications are much preferred to all other communication methods. However, two-way communications require considerations of cost, signal access, transmission rates, interference, and methods for keeping sensor and communication power loops separate. Two-way communications are frequently impossible (no service) or impractical, expensive, or power consumptive. Two-way methods (cellular, land line, radio, Internet) require smaller up-front costs as compared to other methods of communication and have variable recurrent costs, starting at zero. Satellite links work everywhere (except when blocked by trees or cliffs) and are quite reliable but are one-way (from station to host server) and relatively slow, allow no re-transmissions, and require high up-front costs ($3–4K) but no recurrent costs. Communications technology is changing constantly and requires vigilant attention by maintenance personnel.

1.4.6. Quality Assurance and Quality Control

Quality control and quality assurance are issues at every step through the entire sequence of sensing, communication, storage, retrieval, and display of environmental data. Quality assurance is an umbrella concept that covers all data collection and processing (start-to-finish) and ensures that credible information is available to the end user. Quality control has a more limited scope and is defined by the International Standards Organization as "the operational techniques and activities that are used to satisfy quality requirements." The central problem can be better appreciated if we approach quality control in the following way.

- Quality control is the evaluation, assessment, and rehabilitation of imperfect data by utilizing other imperfect data.

The quality of the data only decreases with time once the observation is made. The best and most effective quality control, therefore, consists in making high-quality measurements from the start and then successfully transmitting the measurements to a data storage site. Once the data are received from a monitoring station, a series of checks with increasing complexity can be applied, ranging from single-element checks (self-consistency) to multiple-element checks (inter-sensor consistency) to multiple-station/single-element checks (inter-station consistency). Suitable ancillary data (battery voltages, data ranges for all measurements, etc.) can prove extremely useful in diagnosing problems.

There is rarely a single technique in quality control procedures that will work satisfactorily for all situations. These procedures must be tailored to individual station circumstances, data access and storage methods, and climate regimes.

The fundamental issue in quality control centers on the tradeoff between falsely rejecting good data (Type I error) and falsely accepting bad data (Type II error). We cannot reduce the incidence of one type of error without increasing the incidence of the other type. In weather and climate data assessments, Type I errors are deemed far less desirable than Type II errors.

Not all observations are equal in importance. Quality-control procedures are likely to have the greatest difficulty evaluating the most extreme observations, where independent information usually must be sought and incorporated. Quality-control procedures involving more than one station usually involve a great deal of infrastructure with its own (imperfect) error-detection methods, which must be in place before a single value can be evaluated.

1.4.7. Standards

Although there is near-universal recognition of the value in systematic weather and climate measurements, these measurements will have little value unless they conform to accepted standards. There is not a single source for standards for collecting weather and climate data nor a single standard that meets all needs. Measurement standards have been developed by the American Association of State Climatologists (AASC 1985), U.S. Environmental Protection Agency (EPA 1987), World Meteorological Organization (WMO 1983; 2005), Finklin and Fischer (1990), National Wildfire Coordinating Group (2004), and the RAWS program (Bureau of Land Management [BLM] 1997). Variations to these measurement standards also have been offered by instrument makers (e.g., Tanner 1990).

1.4.8. Who Makes the Measurements?

The lands under NPS stewardship provide many excellent locations to host the monitoring of climate by the NPS or other collaborators. Most park units historically have observed weather/climate elements as part of their overall mission. Many of these measurements come from station networks managed by other agencies, with observations taken or overseen by NPS personnel, in some cases, or by collaborators from the other agencies. National Park Service units that are small, lack sufficient resources, or lack sites presenting adequate exposure may benefit by utilizing weather/climate measurements collected from nearly stations.

2.0. Climate Background

Ecosystem processes in the NCBN are strongly governed by climate characteristics (Godfrey et al. 1999; CACO 2001; Stevens et al. 2005). It is essential that NCBN park units have an effective climate monitoring system to track climate changes and to aid in management decisions relating to these changes. These efforts are needed in order to support current vital sign monitoring activities within NCBN park units. The NCBN is currently developing protocols to monitor salt marsh vegetation, nekton, estuarine water quality, and ocean shoreline position, each of which are influenced by climate (CACO 2001; Stevens et al. 2005). It is therefore essential to understand the primary climate characteristics of the NCBN, which are discussed in this chapter.

2.1. Climate and the NCBN Environment

Atmospheric agents (wind, solar radiation, rain, fog, salt spray, deposition, etc.) are important factors governing the activity of organisms, community composition, and the cycling of materials through the ecosystems of the NCBN (Godfrey et al. 1999; CACO 2001; Stevens et al. 2005). Storm surges and their associated winds and waves can alter ocean and estuarine shoreline configurations (Zeigler et al. 1959; Giese and Aubrey 1987; Nordstrom 1992; Nordstrom 2000), and dramatically affect estuarine circulation and sedimentation processes (Aubrey and Speer 1985; Roman et al. 1997). Drought periods or excess precipitation influence seasonal water balance, affecting wetlands, kettle ponds, vernal pools, and groundwater resources (LeBlanc et al. 1986; Portnoy et al. 2001). The effects of atmospheric deposition include the acidification of lakes and streams, nutrient enrichment of coastal waters, depletion of soil nutrients leading to the decline of sensitive habitats, agricultural crop damage, and impacts on ecosystem diversity (Hinga et al. 1991; Jaworski et al. 1997).

The NCBN parks contain critical coastal and wetland habitat for rare and endangered species. These areas also act as important migratory corridors for various animal species (Stevens et al. 2005). Imposed on these characteristics is a long history of human uses in the NCBN region. These natural systems are, however, being stressed by ongoing population growth in the northeastern U.S., which is occurring particularly in coastal areas (Culliton et al. 1990; Stevens et al. 2005). Examples of such stresses include atmospheric pollutant deposition and habitat fragmentation, all of which have negative impacts on the region's biodiversity (Stevens et al. 2005). Climate changes associated with these influences may include extensions of urban heat island effects and altered precipitation patterns due to spatial pollutant patterns and land use changes (NAST 2001).

As a result of human stresses, the natural systems of the NCBN are likely becoming more vulnerable to damages from extreme storm events. These storm events include tropical cyclones, which occur during the summer and fall seasons, and nor'easters, which are common from fall to spring. In some rare circumstances during the fall months, tropical cyclones have combined with extratropical low pressure centers to create exceptionally strong nor'easter storms. An example of this is the well-known "Perfect Storm" in October, 1991, where an extratropical low combined with energy from Hurricane Grace to create a very powerful nor'easter. Winds and heavy precipitation from these storms are important disturbance factors for the NCBN ecosystems, particularly in the ongoing geomorphology of coastal areas (Stevens et al. 2005). During the winter months, nor'easters can bring either heavy snow or flooding rain, depending on the track of the primary low pressure centers associated with these nor'easters. These extreme events can cause disturbances which make plant and animal communities more susceptible to diseases and insect infestations. They also introduce further habitat fragmentation in areas which are already significantly fragmented by human uses. Tropical cyclones, for instance, have been known to introduce large-scale disturbances into eastern U.S. ecosystems (Lugo and Scatena 1996; Lugo 2000). During any time of the year, but particularly during the winter months, devastating flooding events can also be driven by nor'easter storms (NAST 2001).

Instrumental records of the climate of the eastern U.S. indicate that the region has experienced significant positive trends in temperature and especially precipitation over the last century (Hughes et al. 1992; Karl et al. 1996b; Karl and Knight 1998; NAST 2001). While the temperature trends for the eastern U.S. show some of the least warming (even slight cooling in southern Pennsylvania) throughout the U.S., a general warming is still evident. For instance, the period of time where snowpack is present on the ground has decreased by 7 days over the last 50 years (Karl et al. 1993; Groisman et al. 2000; NAST 2001). The precipitation trends in the eastern U.S. have shown strong increases over the last century, with this trend projected to continue into the future (Karl et al. 1996b; Karl and Knight 1998; NAST 2001). It is expected that one of the results of future climate changes in the eastern U.S. will be an increase in the number of ice storms (NAST 2001). There may also be significant changes in the number and intensity of extreme events such as hurricanes and nor'easters (Groisman et al. 2000). These changes will influence (both adversely and constructively), to varying degrees, the natural systems of the NCBN (Shaver et al. 2000).

2.2. Spatial Variability

Mean annual temperatures in the NCBN (Figure 2.1) generally decrease from south to north. These temperatures range from close to 14°C near Colonial National Historical Park (COLO) to about 9°C in CACO. Compared to locations further inland, temperatures in the NCBN are significantly moderated by the presence of the Atlantic Ocean. This can clearly be seen in the average minimum temperatures in January (Figure 2.2), which are generally about 5-10°C warmer than the corresponding minima further inland. Along the coast, January minimums are generally between -2°C in the south to almost -7°C in the north. Summers in the region are warm and humid. July mean maximum temperatures in the NCBN (Figure 2.3) range from 22°C in CACO to just over 30°C near COLO. Temperatures in the coastal parks are again moderated by the Atlantic Ocean, as they are in winter. The effect of this moderation, however, is not as obvious during the summer as it is during the winter. The greatest moderation effects are indicated along CACO, where July maxima are generally 5-10°C cooler than land areas immediately to the west.

Mean annual precipitation in the NCBN lies between 1000 and 1200 mm (Figure 2.4). These values do not differ appreciably from locations further inland.

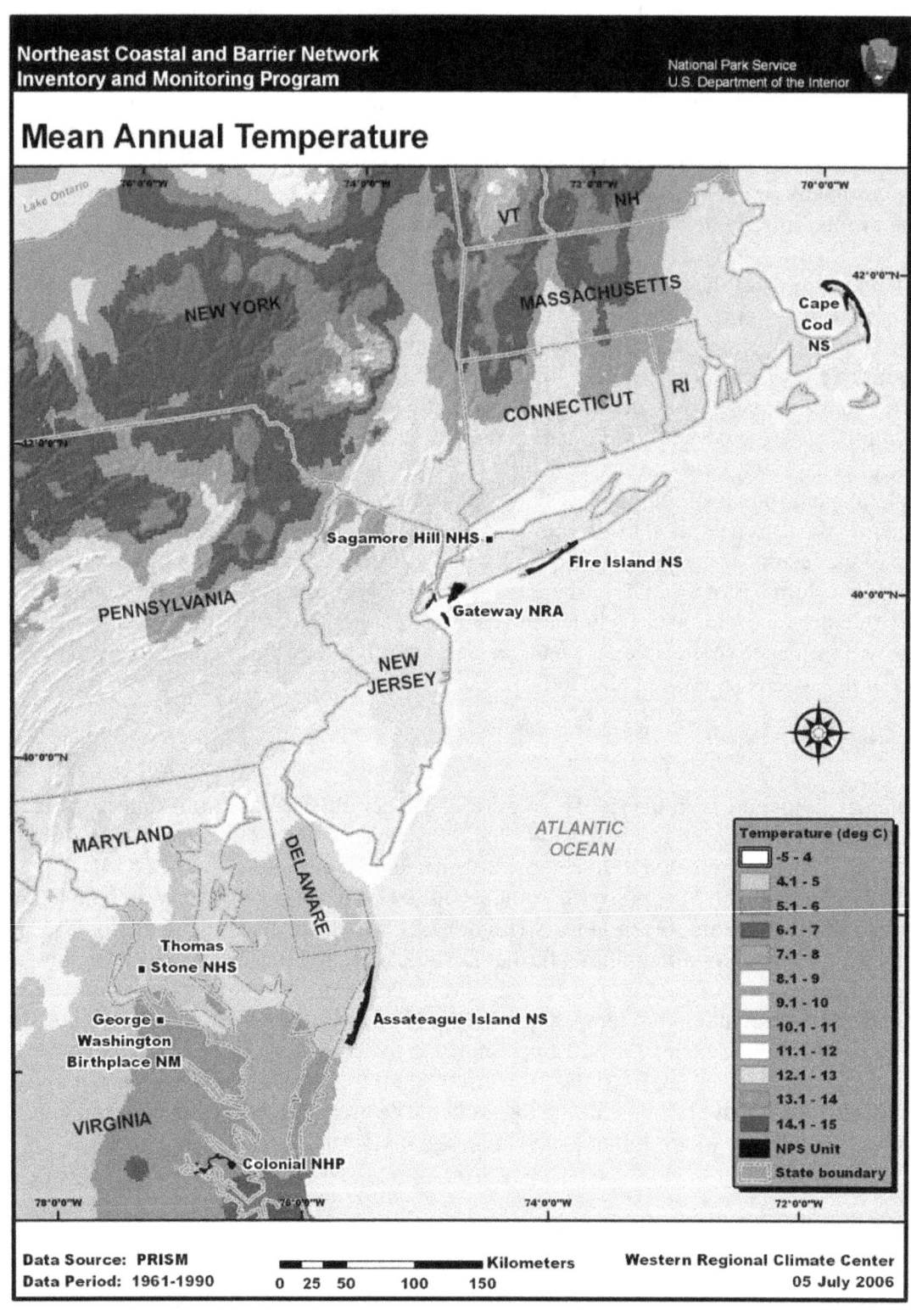

Figure 2.1. Mean annual temperature, 1961–1990, for the NCBN.

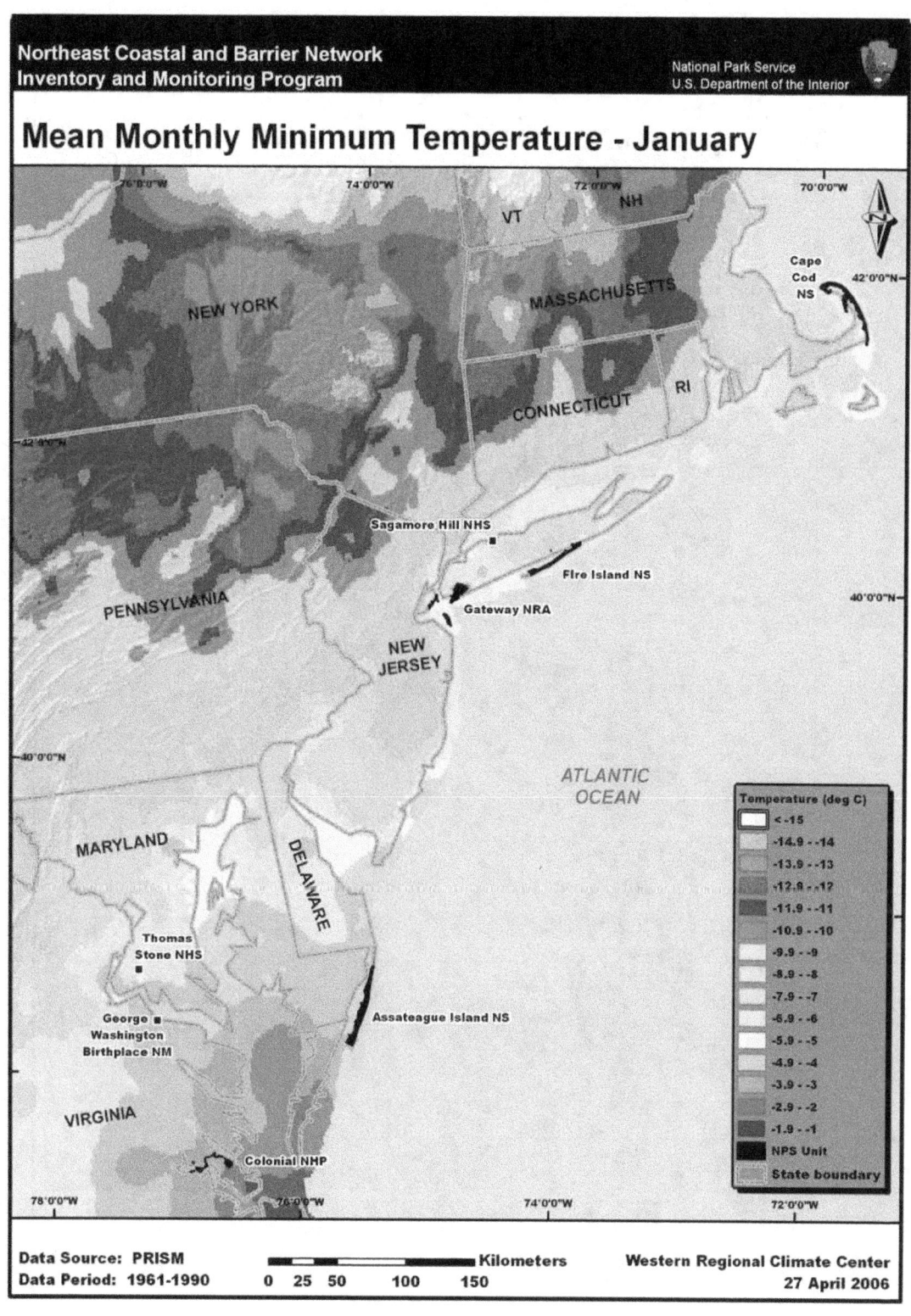

Figure 2.2. Mean January minimum temperature, 1961-1990, for the NCBN.

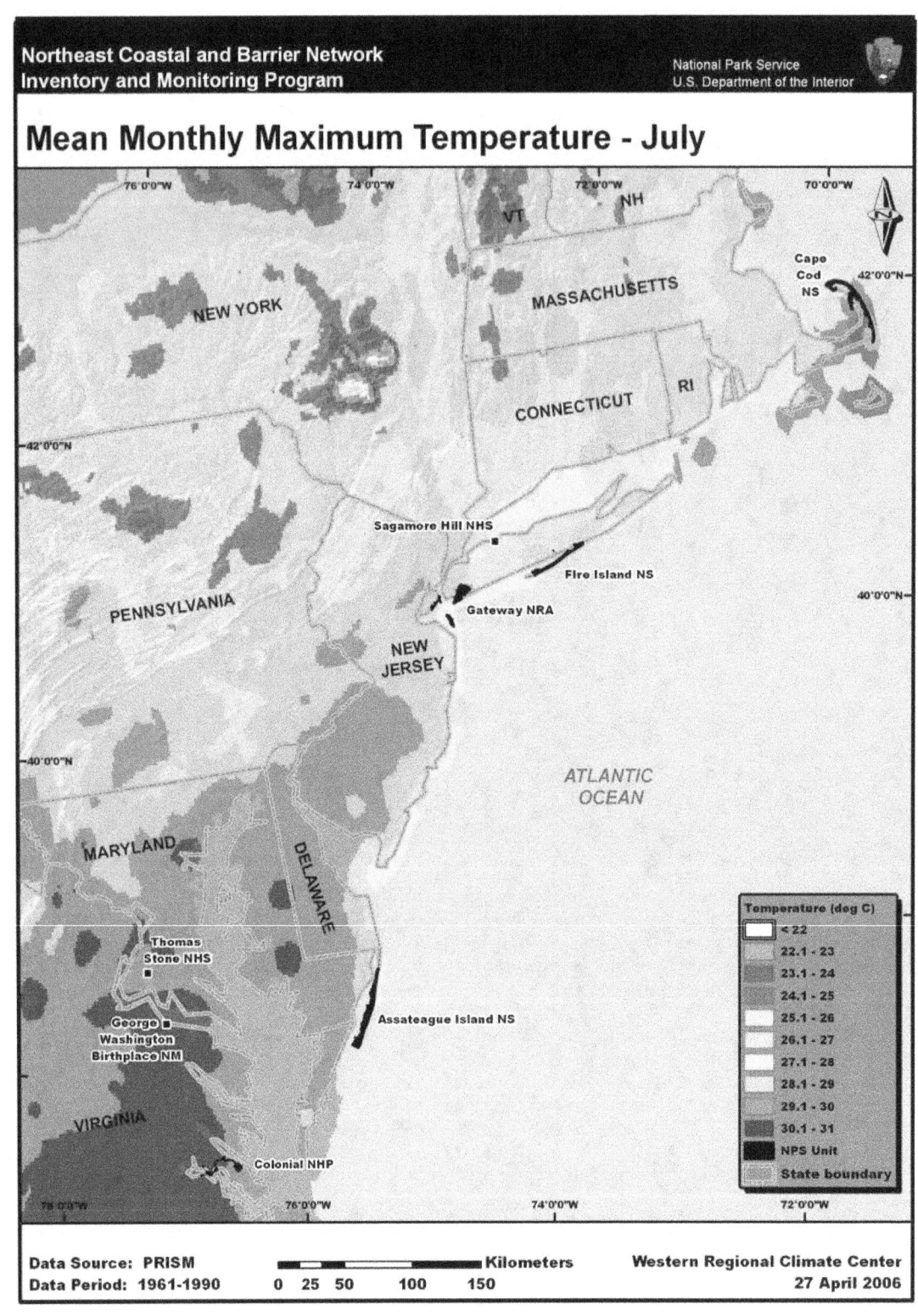

Figure 2.3. Mean July maximum temperature, 1961-1990, for the NCBN.

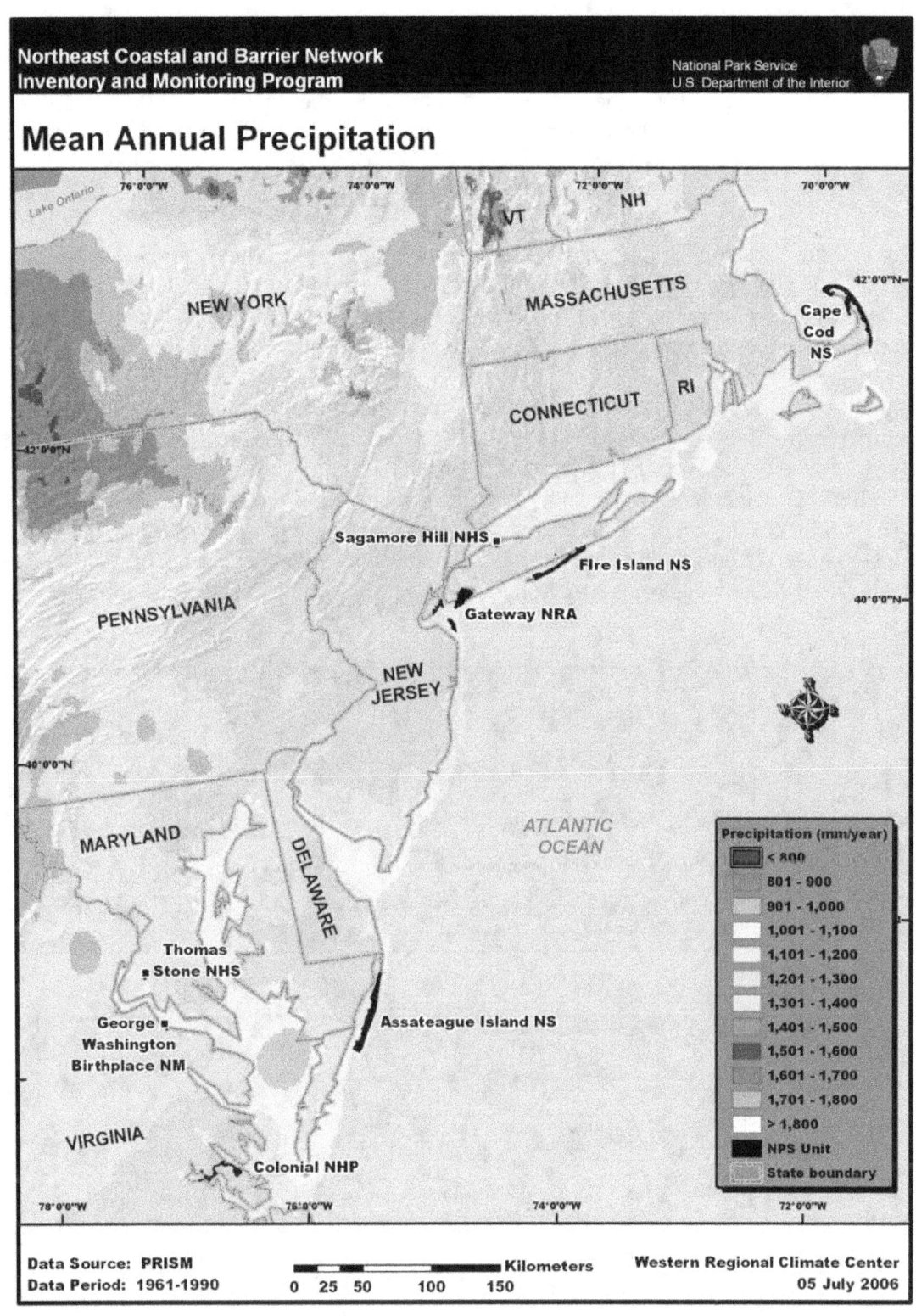

Figure 2.4. Mean annual precipitation, 1961-1990, for the NCBN.

2.3. Temporal Variability

Monthly precipitation characteristics (Figure 2.5) show that precipitation is a common occurrence throughout the year. Precipitation is greater during the summer months in the southern park units and greater in the winter months in the northern park units. Precipitation trends in the eastern U.S. have shown strong increases in precipitation over the last century (Karl et al. 1996b; Karl and Knight 1998; NAST 2001). In the NCBN, this is readily apparent (Figure 2.6).

There are marked variations in the temporal temperature patterns exhibited across the NCBN (Figure 2.7). The southern parts of the NCBN, such as the Tidewater region of Virginia, show temperatures that have increased by 0.5°C or less. In contrast, coastal areas to the north and east (e.g. coastal Massachusetts) have seen temperatures rise by at least 1°C.

About three tropical storms and/or hurricanes have made landfall in the U.S. each year over the past century (Lyons 2004). Most of these storms that make landfall in the U.S. originate either in the Gulf of Mexico or the Western Caribbean (Lyons 2004). Hurricanes have generally made landfall in the U.S. at a rate of just under one per year over the past century (Smith 1999; Lyons 2004). The number of these storms that reach middle and northern portions of the eastern U.S. has been very sporadic during this time period but the events, when they do occur, tend to do so in clusters. These clusters of storms occur on time scales of a couple decades (Smith 1999).

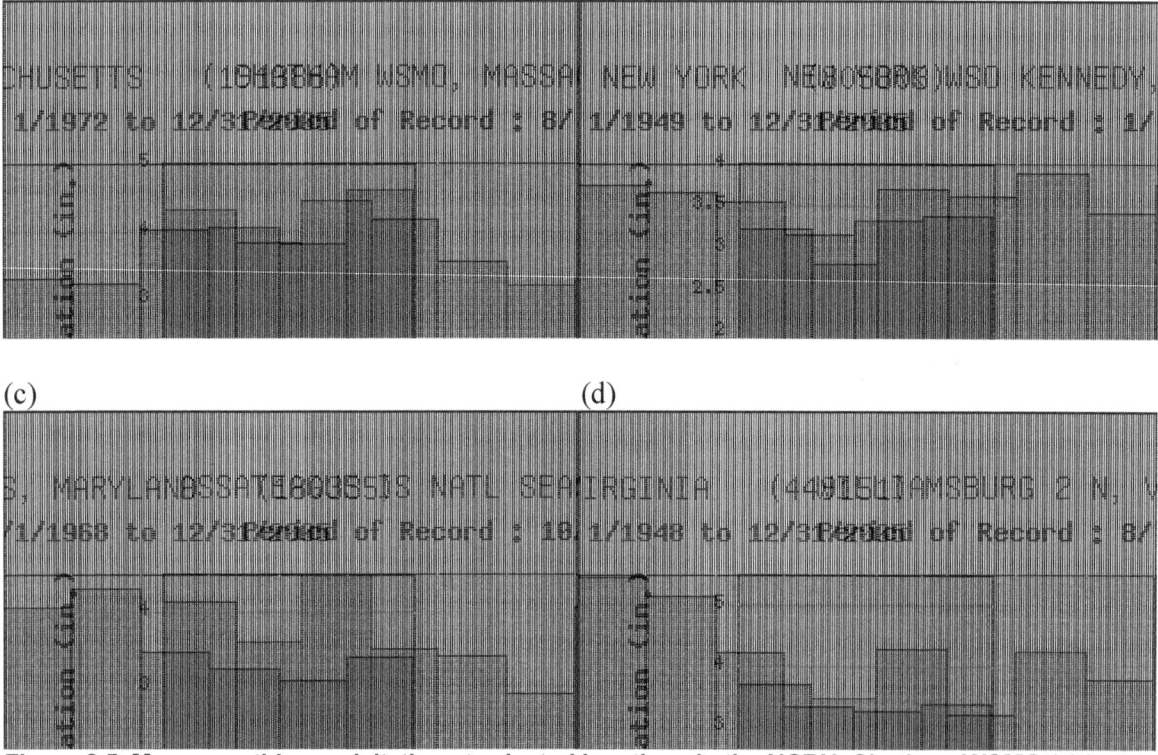

Figure 2.5. Mean monthly precipitation at selected locations in the NCBN. Chatham WSMO (a) is the northernmost location, while Williamsburg 2 N (d) is the southernmost location.

16

(a)

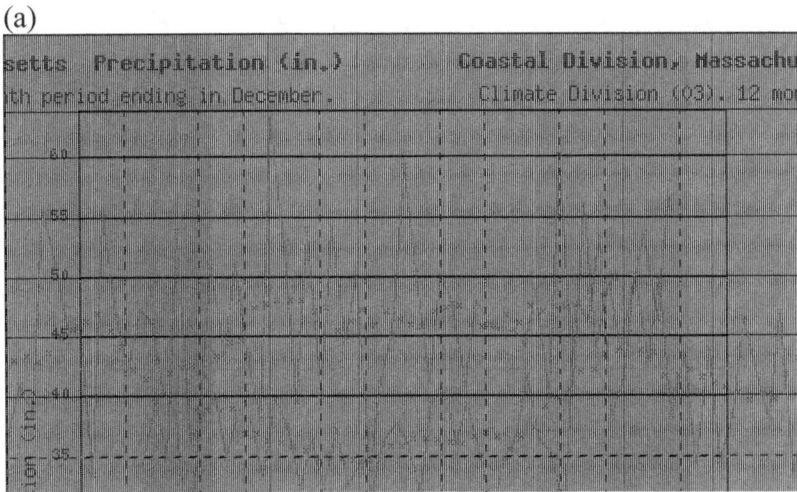

(b)

(c)

Figure 2.6. Precipitation time series, 1895-2005, for coastal Massachusetts (a), coastal New York (b) and the Tidewater region of Virginia (c). Twelve-month average precipitation ending in December (red), 10-year running mean (blue), mean (green), and plus/minus one standard deviation (green dotted line).

(a)

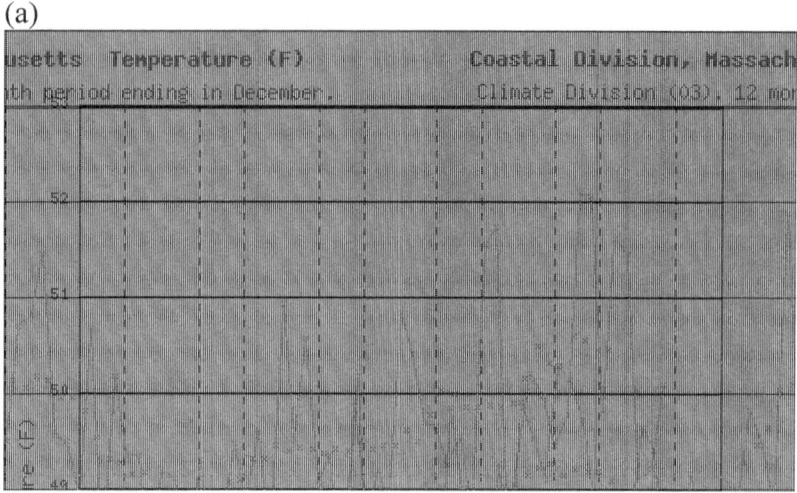

(b)

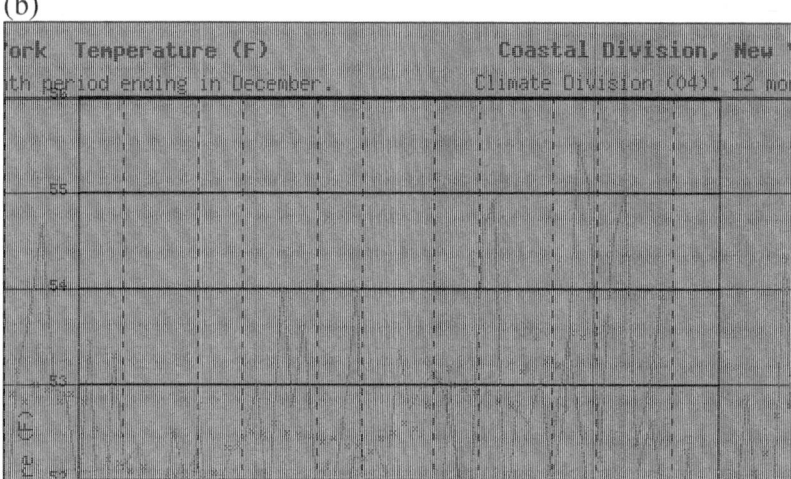

(c)

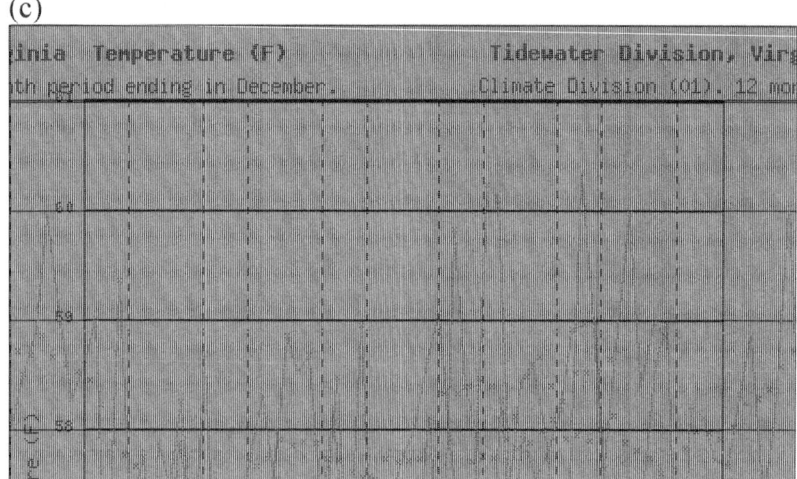

Figure 2.7. Temperature time series, 1895-2005, for coastal Massachusetts (a), coastal New York (b) and the Tidewater region of Virginia (c). Twelve-month average temperature ending in December (red), 10-year running mean (blue), mean (green), and plus/minus one standard deviation (green dotted line).

2.4. Parameter Regression on Independent Slopes Model (PRISM)

The climate maps presented here were generated using the Parameter Regression on Independent Slopes Model (PRISM). This model is maintained by PRISM Group at Oregon State University (http://www.ocs.orst.edu/prism) and was developed to address the extreme spatial and elevation gradients exhibited by the climate of the western U.S. (Daly et al. 1994; 2002; Gibson et al. 2002; Doggett et al. 2004). Originally, this model was developed to describe spatial climate variability at scales that match available land-cover maps, to assist in ecologic modeling. Spatial climate data sets generated from PRISM are now widely used for Geographic Information Systems applications. The PRISM technique accounts for the scale-dependent effects of topography on mean values of climate elements. Elevation provides the first-order constraint for the mapped climate fields, with slope and orientation (aspect) providing second-order constraints. The model has been enhanced gradually to address inversions, coast/land gradients, and climate patterns in small-scale trapping basins. Monthly climate fields are generated by PRISM to account for seasonal variations in elevation gradients in climate elements. These monthly climate fields then can be combined into seasonal and annual climate fields. Since PRISM maps are grid maps, they do not replicate point values but rather, for a given grid cell, represent the grid-cell average of the climate variable in question at the average elevation for that cell. The model relies on observed surface and upper-air measurements to estimate spatial climate fields.

3.0. Methods

Having discussed the climatic characteristics of the NCBN, we now present the procedures that were used to obtain information for weather/climate stations within the NCBN. This information was obtained from various sources, as mentioned in the following paragraphs. Retrieval of station metadata constituted a major component of this work.

3.1. Criteria for Locating Stations

To identify stations for each park unit in the NCBN, we selected only those that were located in NCBN park units or within 30 km of a NCBN park-unit boundary. We selected this buffer distance in order to ensure the inclusion of a sufficient number of both manual and automated stations in and near the park units in the NCBN. More specific buffering procedures might be considered to account for differences between coastal and inland weather and climate patterns. For example, a more restricted buffer could be considered for barrier-island park units such as FIIS, focusing only on weather/climate stations located on the barrier island and the immediately surrounding marine areas. These buffering procedures, however, are beyond the scope of this report.

The station locator maps presented in Chapter 4 were designed to show clearly the spatial distributions of all major weather/climate station networks in the NCBN. We recognize that other mapping formats may be more suitable for other specific needs.

3.2. Metadata Retrieval

A key component of station inventories is determining the kinds of observations that have been conducted over time, by whom, and in what manner; when each type of observation began and ended; and whether these observations are still being conducted. Metadata about the observational process generally consist of a series of vignettes that apply to time intervals and, therefore, constitute a *history* rather than a single snapshot. This report has relied on metadata records from three sources: (a) Western Regional Climate Center (WRCC), (b) NPS personnel, and (c) other knowledgeable personnel, such as state climate office staff. Metadata (Table 3.1) have been obtained as completely as possible for weather/climate stations in and near the NCBN park units. Station metadata are not complete for some of the stations listed in Chapter 4. The most commonly lacking metadata include contact information and specific information regarding the siting characteristics of a station (slope, aspect, photographic documentation, etc.). An expanded list of relevant metadata fields for this inventory is provided in Appendix E.

Table 3.1. Primary metadata fields for weather/climate stations within the NCBN. Explanations are given as appropriate.

Metadata Field	Notes
Station name	Station name associated with network listed in "Climate Network."
Latitude	Numerical value (units: see coordinate units).
Longitude	Numerical value (units: see coordinate units).
Coordinate units	Latitude/longitude (units: decimal degrees, degree-minute-second, etc.).
Datum	Datum used as basis for coordinates: WGS 84, NAD 83, etc.
Elevation	Elevation of station above mean sea level (m).
Slope	Slope of ground surface below station (degrees).
Aspect	Azimuth that ground surface below station faces.
Climate division	NOAA climate division where station is located. Climate divisions are NOAA-specified zones sharing similar climate and hydrology characteristics.
Country	Country where station is located.
State	State where station is located.
County	County where station is located.
Weather/climate network	Primary weather/climate network the station belongs to (RAWS, Clean Air Status and Trends Network [CASTNet], etc.).
NPS unit code	Four-letter code identifying park unit where station resides.
NPS unit name	Full name of park unit.
NPS unit type	National park, national monument, etc.
UTM zone	If UTM is the only coordinate system available.
Location notes	Useful information not already included in "station narrative."
Climate variables	Temperature, precipitation, etc.
Installation date	Date of station installation.
Removal date	Date of station removal.
Station photograph	Digital image of station.
Photograph date	Date photograph was taken.
Photographer	Name of person who took the photograph.
Station narrative	Anything related to general site description; may include site exposure, characteristics of surrounding vegetation, driving directions, etc.
Contact name	Name of the person involved with station operation.
Organization	Group or agency affiliation of contact person.
Contact type	Designation that identifies contact person as the station owner, observer, maintenance person, data manager, etc.
Position/job title	Official position/job title of contact person.
Address	Address of contact person.
E-mail address	E-mail address of contact person.
Phone	Phone number of contact person (and extension if available).
Contact notes	Other information needed to reach contact person.

The initial metadata sources for this report were stored at WRCC. This regional climate center (RCC) acts as a working repository of many western climate records, including the main networks outlined in this section. The WRCC conducts live and periodic data collection (ingests) from all major national and western weather/climate networks. These networks include the COOP network, the SAO network, the interagency RAWS network, and various smaller networks. The WRCC is expanding its capability to ingest information from other networks as resources permit and usefulness dictates. This center has relied heavily on historic archives (in many cases supplemented with live ingests) to assess the quantity (not necessarily quality) of data available for NPS I&M network applications.

The primary source of metadata at WRCC is the Applied Climate Information System (ACIS), a joint effort among RCCs and other NOAA entities. Metadata for NCBN weather/climate stations identified from the ACIS database are available in file "NCBN__from_ACIS.tar.gz" (see Appendix F). Historic metadata pertaining to major climate- and weather-observing systems in the U.S. are stored in ACIS where metadata are linked to the observed data. A distributed system, ACIS is synchronized among the RCCs. Mainstream software is utilized, including Postgress, Python™, and Java™ programming languages; CORBA®-compliant network software; and industry-standard, nonproprietary hardware and software. Metadata and data for all major national climate and weather networks have been entered into the ACIS database. For this project, the available metadata from many smaller networks also have been entered but in most cases the actual data have not yet been entered. Data sets are in the NetCDF (Network Common Data Form) format, but the design allows for integration with legacy systems, including non-NetCDF files (used at WRCC) and additional metadata (added for this project). The ACIS also supports a suite of products to visualize or summarize data from these data sets. National climate-monitoring maps are updated daily using the ACIS data feed. The developmental phases of ACIS have utilized metadata supplied by the NCDC and NWS with many tens of thousands of entries, screened as well as possible for duplications, mistakes, and omissions.

In addition to obtaining NCBN weather/climate station metadata from ACIS, metadata were obtained from NPS staff at the NCBN office in Boston, Massachusetts. Conner and Albert (2004) and CACO (2001) have provided preliminary inventories of weather and climate stations in the NCBN. There is some overlap between the ACIS and NCBN metadata sets. The metadata provided from the NCBN office are available in file "NCBN_NPS.tar.gz". In addition, we have relied on information supplied at various times in the past by NCDC and the Northeast Regional Climate Center (NERCC), along with the state climate offices of New Jersey and Delaware (Table 3.2).

Table 3.2. Additional sources of weather and climate metadata for the NCBN.

Name	Position	Phone Number	Email Address
Keith Eggleston	Research Support, NERCC	(607)255-1749	kle1@cornell.edu
David Robinson	New Jersey State Climatologist	(732)445-4741	drobins@rci.rutgers.edu
David Legates	Delaware State Climatologist	(928)556-9161	legates@udel.edu

Two types of information have been used to complete the climate station inventory for NCBN.

- Station inventories: Information about operational procedures, latitude/longitude, elevation, measured elements, measurement frequency, sensor types, exposures, ground cover and vegetation, data-processing details, network, purpose, and managing individual or agency, etc.

- Data inventories: Information about measured data values including start and end dates, completeness, properties of data gaps, representation of missing data, flagging systems, how special circumstances are denoted in the data record, etc.

This is not a straightforward process. Extensive searches are typically required to develop historic station and data inventories. Both types of inventories frequently contain information gaps. Sources of information for these inventories frequently are difficult to recover or are undocumented and unreliable. In many cases, the actual weather/climate data available from different sources are not linked directly to metadata records. To the extent that actual data can be acquired (rather than just metadata), it is possible to cross-check these records and perform additional assessments based on the amount and completeness of the data.

Certain types of weather/climate networks that possess any of the following attributes have not been considered for inclusion in the inventory:

- Private networks with proprietary access and/or inability to obtain or provide sufficient metadata.
- Private weather enthusiasts (often with high-quality data) whose metadata are not available and whose data are not readily accessible.
- Unofficial observers supplying data to the NWS (lack of access to current data and historic archives; lack of metadata).
- Networks having no available historic data.
- Networks having poor-quality metadata.
- Networks having poor access to metadata.
- Real-time networks having poor access to real-time data.

Previous inventory efforts at WRCC have shown that for the weather networks identified in the preceding list, in light of the need for quality data to track weather and climate, the resources required (often very substantial) and difficulty encountered in obtaining metadata or data are prohibitively large.

23

4.0. Station Inventory

An objective of this report is to show the locations of weather/climate stations for the NCBN region in relation to the boundaries of the NCBN park units. A station does not have to be within park boundaries to provide useful data and information for a park unit.

4.1. Climate and Weather Networks

Most stations in the NCBN region are associated with at least one of nine major weather/climate networks (Table 4.1). Brief descriptions of each weather/climate network are provided below (see Appendix G for greater detail).

Table 4.1. Weather/climate networks represented within the NCBN.

Acronym	Name
COOP	NWS Cooperative Observer Program
CWOP	Citizen Weather Observer Program
GPMP	Gaseous Pollutant Monitoring Program
GPS-MET	NOAA ground-based GPS meteorology
POMS	Portable Ozone Monitoring System
RAWS	Remote Automated Weather Station Network
SAO	NWS/FAA Surface Airways Observations Network
WBAN	Weather Bureau Army Navy
WX4U	Weather For You Network

4.1.1. NWS Cooperative Observer Program (COOP)

The COOP network has been a foundation of the U.S. climate program for decades and continues to play an important role. Manual measurements are made by volunteers and consist of daily maximum and minimum temperatures, observation-time temperature, daily precipitation, daily snowfall, and snow depth. When blended with NWS measurements, the data set is known as SOD, or "Summary of the Day." The quality of data from COOP sites ranges from excellent to modest.

4.1.2. Citizen Weather Observer Program (CWOP)

The CWOP network consists primarily of automated weather stations operated by private citizens who have either an Internet connection and/or a wireless Ham radio setup. Data from CWOP stations are specifically intended for use in research, education, and homeland security activities. Although standard meteorological elements such as temperature, precipitation, and wind are measured at all CWOP stations, station characteristics do vary, including sensor types and site exposure.

4.1.3. NPS Gaseous Pollutant Monitoring Program (GPMP)

The GPMP network measures hourly meteorological data in support of pollutant monitoring activities. Measured elements include temperature, precipitation, humidity, wind, solar radiation, and surface wetness. These data are of high quality, with records extending up to 1-2 decades in length.

4.1.4. NOAA Ground-Based GPS Meteorology (GPS-MET)

The GPS-MET network is the first network of its kind dedicated to GPS meteorology (see Duan et al. 1996). GPS meteorology utilizes the radio signals broadcast by the satellite Global Positioning System for atmospheric remote sensing. GPS meteorology applications have evolved along two paths: ground-based (Bevis et al. 1992) and space-based (Yuan et al. 1993). For more information, please see Appendix G. The stations identified in this inventory are all ground-based. The GPS-MET network was developed in response to the need for improved moisture observations to support weather forecasting, climate monitoring, and other research activities. The primary goals of this network are to measure atmospheric water vapor using ground-based GPS receivers, facilitate the operational use of these data, and encourage usage of GPS meteorology for atmospheric research and other applications. GPS-MET is a collaboration between NOAA and several other governmental and university organizations and institutions. Ancillary meteorological observations at GPS-MET stations include temperature, relative humidity, and pressure.

4.1.5. Portable Ozone Monitoring System (POMS)

The POMS network is operated by the NPS Air Resources Division. Sites are intended primarily for short-term (1-5 years) monitoring of near-surface atmospheric ozone levels in remote locations. Measured meteorological elements include temperature, precipitation, wind, relative humidity, and solar radiation.

4.1.6. Remote Automated Weather Station Network (RAWS)

The RAWS network is administered through many land management agencies, particularly the BLM and the Forest Service. Hourly meteorology elements are measured and include temperature, wind, humidity, solar radiation, barometric pressure, fuel temperature, and precipitation (when temperatures are above freezing). The fire community is the primary client for RAWS data. These sites are remote and data typically are transmitted via GOES (Geostationary Operational Environmental Satellite). Some sites operate all winter. Most data records for RAWS sites began during or after the mid-1980s.

4.1.7. NWS/FAA Surface Airways Observations Network (SAO)

These stations are located usually at major airports and military bases. Almost all SAO sites are automated. The hourly data measured at these sites include temperature, precipitation, humidity, wind, pressure, sky cover, ceiling, visibility, and current weather. Most data records begin during or after the 1940s, and these data are generally of high quality.

4.1.8. Weather Bureau Army Navy (WBAN)

This is a station identification system rather than a true weather/climate network and is not discussed in Appendix G. A brief description of WBAN is provided here. Stations identified with WBAN are largely historical stations that reported meteorological observations on the WBAN weather observation forms that were common during the early and middle parts of the 20th Century. The use of WBAN numbers to identify stations was one of the first attempts in the U.S. to use a coordinated station numbering scheme between several weather station networks, such as the SAO and COOP networks.

4.1.9. Weather For You Network (WX4U)

The WX4U network is a nationwide collection of weather stations run by local observers. Data quality varies with site. Standard meteorological elements are measured and usually include temperature, precipitation, wind, and humidity.

4.1.10. Other Networks

In addition to the major networks mentioned above, there are various networks that are operated for specific purposes by specific organizations or governmental agencies or scientific research projects. These networks could be present within the NCBN but have not been identified in this report. Some of the commonly used networks include the following:

- NOAA upper-air stations
- Federal and state departments of transportation
- National Science Foundation Long-Term Ecologic Research Network
- U.S. Department of Energy Surface Radiation Budget Network (Surfrad)
- U.S. Geological Survey (USGS) hydrologic stations
- Park-specific-monitoring networks and stations
- Other research or project networks having many possible owners

4.2. Station Locations

The major weather/climate networks in the NCBN (discussed in Section 4.1) have at most a few stations that are at or inside each park unit (Table 4.2). Cape Cod National Seashore has the most weather/climate stations located inside park boundaries (8), while the NCBN park units in New York City and on Long Island (FIIS, GATE, and SAHI) have the most weather/climate stations both in and near park boundaries. In all, we have identified 20 weather/climate stations inside the park units of the NCBN.

Lists of stations have been compiled for the NCBN. A station does not have to be within the boundaries to provide useful data and information regarding the park unit in question. Some might be physically *within* the administrative or political boundaries, whereas others might be just outside, or even some distance away, but would be *nearby* in behavior and representativeness. What constitutes "useful" and "representative" are also significant questions, whose answers can vary according to application, type of element, period of record, procedural or methodological observation conventions, and the like.

Table 4.2. Number of stations within and nearby NCBN park units. Numbers are listed by park unit and by weather/climate network. Figures in parentheses indicate number of stations within park boundaries.

Network	ASIS	CACO	COLO	FIIS	GATE	GEWA	SAHI	THST
COOP	14(2)	8(4)	13(0)	15(0)	59(2)	13(0)	38(0)	21(0)
CWOP	0(0)	5(0)	11(0)	42(1)	54(0)	7(0)	34(0)	15(0)
GPMP	0(0)	1(1)	0(0)	0(0)	0(0)	0(0)	0(0)	0(0)
GPS-MET	0(0)	0(0)	1(0)	1(0)	3(1)	0(0)	1(0)	0(0)
POMS	1(0)	0(0)	0(0)	0(0)	0(0)	0(0)	0(0)	0(0)
RAWS	3(1)	1(1)	0(0)	3(0)	8(0)	0(0)	1(0)	1(0)
SAO	5(0)	7(2)	6(0)	6(0)	13(3)	1(0)	8(0)	3(0)
WBAN	3(1)	1(0)	1(0)	5(0)	8(1)	0(0)	4(0)	0(0)
WX4U	0(0)	1(0)	1(0)	6(0)	13(0)	0(0)	6(0)	1(0)
Total	26(4)	24(8)	33(0)	78(1)	158(7)	21(0)	102(0)	41(0)

4.2.1. Cape Cod National Seashore

We have identified eight weather/climate stations that are located within Cape Cod National Seashore (CACO; Figure 4.1). Four these sites are manual sites, while four are automated (Table 4.3). The four manual stations are all COOP stations; however, only one of these stations (Provincetown 3 NW) is currently active. The COOP site "Provincetown 3 NW" has operated since 1893, providing the longest data record in the CACO region. Most of the automated stations in CACO began operating in the 1980s or later, including the GPMP and RAWS stations inside CACO. However, the SAO station "Race Point Light Stn" has a period of record that goes back to 1958.

In addition to these stations, there are several active and historical stations that were noted to us by NPS (CACO 2001; Conner and Albert 2004). Data and metadata availability for these stations could not be verified; therefore, the stations are listed in Appendix H. There are two weather stations near Truro in addition to the COOP station "North Truro". These include a station operated by the Fire Management Office and a station at Provincelands Visitor Center in Provincetown, Massachusetts, operated by the Massachusetts Department of Environmental Protection. Both stations measure the meteorological elements of temperature, precipitation, relative humidity, wind speed and direction, temperature, and fuel moisture. The Truro station operated by the state of Massachusetts also hosts a NADP station. There is a manual fire weather station at the South District Fire Station in South Wellfleet, Massachusetts. There are two rain gauges, one at Duck Pond (Wellfleet) and the other near the Salt Pond Visitor Center (Eastham).

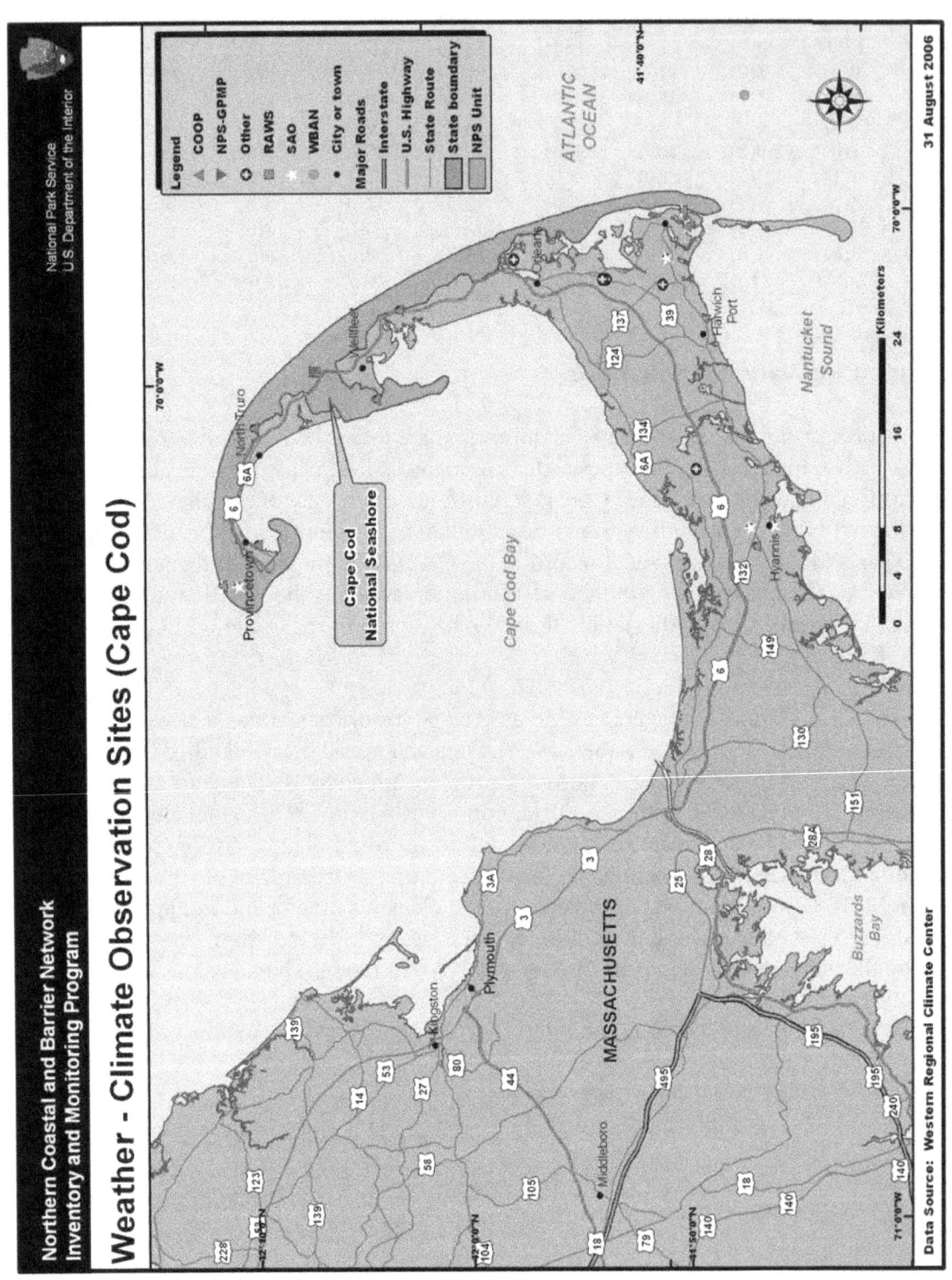

Figure 4.1. Station locations for Cape Cod National Seashore.

Table 4.3. Weather/climate stations for Cape Cod National Seashore. Stations inside park units and within 30 km of the park unit boundary are included. Missing entries are indicated by "M".

Name	Lat.	Lon.	Elev. (m)	Network	Start	End	In Park?
Cape Cod National Seashore (CACO)							
North Truro	42.033	-70.067	42	COOP	6/1/1948	9/9/1954	YES
Provincetown 3 NW	42.083	-70.217	12	COOP	1/1/1893	Present	YES
South Wellfleet	41.900	-69.983	15	COOP	7/1/1963	1/1/1978	YES
Wellfleet	41.933	-70.067	24	COOP	6/25/1958	4/12/1967	YES
Fox Bottom Area	41.976	-70.025	41	GPMP	4/1/1987	Present	YES
Cape Cod	41.975	-70.025	46	RAWS	4/1/2003	Present	YES
Provincetown Muni. AP	42.072	-70.221	2	SAO	9/21/1989	Present	YES
Race Point Light Stn	42.083	-70.217	12	SAO	9/1/1958	Present	YES
Chatham CG	41.667	-69.950	12	COOP	3/1/1949	9/1/1972	NO
Chatham WSMO	41.667	-69.967	15	COOP	8/2/1972	Present	NO
Hyannis	41.667	-70.300	15	COOP	6/1/1948	Present	NO
Provincetown	42.050	-70.183	6	COOP	9/1/1954	7/1/2005	NO
CW3570 Orleans	41.804	-69.960	15	CWOP	M	Present	NO
CW3349 South Orleans	41.737	-70.001	14	CWOP	M	Present	NO
K1ui S.Chatham	41.695	-70.019	12	CWOP	M	Present	NO
CW1321 Brewster	41.746	-70.082	31	CWOP	M	Present	NO
CW1444 Hyannis	41.700	-70.210	30	CWOP	M	Present	NO
Chatham CG	41.667	-69.950	12	SAO	3/2/1943	Present	NO
Chatham Muni. AP	41.688	-69.993	21	SAO	5/11/1962	Present	NO
Chatham WSMO	41.667	-69.967	15	SAO	1/1/1970	Present	NO
Hyannis Barnstable Muni. AP	41.669	-70.280	17	SAO	6/1/1937	Present	NO
Hyannis NAAF	41.650	-70.283	13	SAO	12/1/1943	5/31/1944	NO
Pollock Rip Lightship	41.600	-69.850	5	WBAN	8/1/1947	6/30/1969	NO
South Orleans	41.740	-70.000	13	WX4U	M	Present	NO

4.2.2. Long Island Park Units

The NCBN park units that are located in the greater New York City metropolitan area and the park units on Long Island are in a very urban setting. Therefore, these park units have numerous weather and climate stations within 30 km of park boundaries (Table 4.4; Figure 4.2). These stations include many long-term manual stations with data records approaching a century or more in length as well as many automated stations such as RAWS and SAO stations. In addition, there are many stations associated with CWOP in this area.

Fire Island National Seashore (FIIS) has only one active station within park boundaries (Table 4.4; Figure 4.2). This is a CWOP station (CW5918 Fair Harbor). However, there are numerous stations that are within 30 km of FIIS. There are seven COOP stations currently active within 30 km of FIIS. The longest period of record of these active stations is found at the "Setauket Strong" COOP station, which has made observations since 1885. The data record has been quite complete throughout much of the station's history, but data have become more intermittent in the past 5-10 years. Other long-term records can be found with the Fire Island COOP station, which has data from 1939, and the Riverhead Research Farm, which has a reliable data record starting from 1938. Automated measurements are readily available from SAO stations located on the west and east ends of FIIS. Just west of FIIS is the SAO station "Fire Island Bay Shor". A nearby RAWS station (Fire Island) was in operation between 1987 and 1991. At the east end of FIIS, the SAO site "Moriches Lightboat S" has provided observations since 1966. A GPS-MET site (East Moriches) and a RAWS site (Eastport) also have provided automated meteorological data at the east edge of FIIS for the last few years. Several dozen CWOP stations are currently operating within 30 km of FIIS. There are also a few stations near FIIS that are associated with the WX4U network.

We have identified no weather/climate stations within SAHI (Table 4.4). However, as with FIIS, there are numerous stations in the vicinity of SAHI. The closest stations to SAHI are just over 5 km away (Figure 4.2). Fourteen active COOP stations have been identified within 30 km of SAHI. Several of these COOP stations have data records that begin before 1950 and a few of these data records actually go back to the 1800s. The previously-discussed COOP site "Setauket Strong" provides useful observations for SAHI. Other COOP stations with data records going back to the 1800s were identified in New York City (Bronx, New York Central Park Obs Belv). The COOP site at New York's Central Park provides a very reliable data record that goes back to 1869. The COOP site "Bronx" has a data record going back to 1894. In addition to the numerous COOP stations around SAHI, there are also numerous CWOP stations within 30 km of SAHI. There are also a few WX4U stations in the vicinity of SAHI.

We have identified one active GPS-MET station and nine active SAO sites within 30 km of SAHI. The closest SAO station to SAHI is "Eaton's Neck Light Stn.", which is about 10 km northeast of SAHI and has operated since 1958. The SAO sites with the longest periods of record are located at New York City's Central Park (1869-present) and the international airports, John F. Kennedy and LaGuardia.

Of all the NCBN units of this section, GATE has the greatest number of weather/climate stations located within 30 km of its boundaries (Table 4.4). Inside GATE, there are two active COOP stations, one active GPS-MET station, and three active SAO stations. Most of these are located in the Jamaica Bay and Sandy Hook units of GATE (Figure 4.2). The longest periods of record come from the COOP and SAO stations named "Sandy Hook Light Stn". Both of these stations have operated since 1903. Additional long-term records inside GATE are available from the SAO site "New York Floyd Benne", which has operated since 1930. Other long-term records are available from the numerous COOP stations outside of GATE. Several of these stations have periods of record that extend back to the late 1800s. The longest period of record is found at New York's Central Park, going back to 1869. There are five active SAO stations located within 30 km of GATE, including those stations located inside park boundaries.

Additional stations have been identified by other climate inventory efforts for GATE (Conner and Albert 2004). However, metadata and data could not be verified for these stations, so these stations are listed in Appendix H. The Sandy Hook unit of GATE apparently has a temperature gauge at the ranger station and a rain gauge in the primary residence area for this unit (Conner and Albert 2004). The Staten Island unit has had a Davis Instruments® weather station on-site and although it is not clear if this station is currently operational, the NPS staff at the Staten

Island unit of GATE intend to keep this station working. The Jamaica Bay unit of GATE has a Davis Instruments® weather station located at the unit ranger station. The siting characteristics of this station have been questionable in the recent past (Conner and Albert 2004).

Table 4.4. Weather/climate stations for NCBN park units on Long Island, New York. Stations inside park units and within 30 km of the park unit boundary are included. Missing entries are indicated by "M".

Name	Lat.	Lon.	Elev. (m)	Network	Start	End	In Park?
Fire Island National Seashore (FIIS)							
CW5918 Fair Harbor	40.638	-73.184	6	CWOP	M	Present	YES
Babylon	40.717	-73.367	15	COOP	3/1/1918	11/30/1974	NO
Brentwood	40.783	-73.250	31	COOP	1/1/1893	8/1/1976	NO
Dix Hills	40.800	-73.300	37	COOP	1/1/1987	10/31/1991	NO
Fire Island	40.633	-73.267	9	COOP	10/1/1939	Present	NO
Holbrook	40.833	-73.083	24	COOP	3/16/1972	12/31/1979	NO
Islip Long Island MacArthur AP	40.794	-73.102	26	COOP	5/1/1948	Present	NO
Lake Ronkonkoma	40.833	-73.133	24	COOP	5/1/1948	3/16/1972	NO
Moriches Lightboat S	40.783	-72.750	3	COOP	4/1/1966	Present	NO
Patchogue 2 N	40.797	-73.001	17	COOP	5/1/1937	11/1/1997	NO
Port Jefferson	40.950	-73.067	3	COOP	11/1/1952	7/31/1976	NO
Riverhead Res Farm	40.962	-72.716	30	COOP	3/1/1938	Present	NO
Sayville Solar Rad	40.767	-73.083	18	COOP	7/1/1952	Present	NO
Setauket 2	40.950	-73.100	12	COOP	M	12/31/1975	NO
Setauket Strong	40.959	-73.105	12	COOP	8/1/1885	Present	NO
Upton	40.871	-72.891	23	COOP	8/1/1948	Present	NO
AB2NE Sayville	40.733	-73.083	6	CWOP	M	Present	NO
CW0028 Great Neck	40.807	-73.737	18	CWOP	M	Present	NO
CW0153 Floral Park	40.730	-73.705	31	CWOP	M	Present	NO
CW0205 West Islip	40.720	-73.306	11	CWOP	M	Present	NO
CW0354 West Islip	40.690	-73.280	1	CWOP	M	Present	NO
CW0411 Brentwood	40.788	-73.251	124	CWOP	M	Present	NO
CW0461 Mt.Sinai	40.940	-73.037	45	CWOP	M	Present	NO
CW0786 Smithtown	40.848	-73.173	20	CWOP	M	Present	NO
CW1379 Shoreham	40.934	-72.883	20	CWOP	M	Present	NO
CW1489 Oakland Gardens	40.740	-73.745	7	CWOP	M	Present	NO
CW1982 Lindenhurst	40.665	-73.378	2	CWOP	M	Present	NO
CW2136 Bohemia	40.763	-73.098	20	CWOP	M	Present	NO
CW2520 Babylon	40.688	-73.333	27	CWOP	M	Present	NO
CW2525 Long Beach	40.588	-73.693	3	CWOP	M	Present	NO
CW2667 Shoreham	40.945	-72.883	125	CWOP	M	Present	NO
CW3335 Bay Shore	40.741	-73.273	15	CWOP	M	Present	NO
CW3340 Valley Stream	40.651	-73.694	7	CWOP	M	Present	NO
CW3615 North Babylon	40.731	-73.324	10	CWOP	M	Present	NO
CW3877 Locust Valley	40.879	-73.592	45	CWOP	M	Present	NO
CW4215 Bellmore	40.676	-73.534	7	CWOP	M	Present	NO

Name	Lat.	Lon.	Elev. (m)	Network	Start	End	In Park?
CW5035 Ronkonkoma	40.810	-73.123	30	CWOP	M	Present	NO
CW5046 Riverhead	40.980	-72.690	40	CWOP	M	Present	NO
CW5086 Greenlawn	40.871	-73.352	68	CWOP	M	Present	NO
CW5202 Mount Sinai	40.925	-73.017	49	CWOP	M	Present	NO
CW5292 Miller Place	40.960	-72.996	40	CWOP	M	Present	NO
CW5400 Rocky Point	40.950	-72.921	46	CWOP	M	Present	NO
CW5573 Mastic Beach	40.778	-72.839	7	CWOP	M	Present	NO
CW5801 Farmingdale	40.726	-73.458	22	CWOP	M	Present	NO
KB2COP Shoreham	40.934	-72.883	34	CWOP	M	Present	NO
KB2COP Shoreham	40.945	-72.883	125	CWOP	M	Present	NO
KB2JOE Brentwood	40.788	-73.252	30	CWOP	M	Present	NO
KB2KMM N. Babylon	40.743	-73.338	14	CWOP	M	Present	NO
KC2KY Centereach	40.872	-73.088	31	CWOP	M	Present	NO
KD1F Farmingville	40.839	-73.060	60	CWOP	M	Present	NO
KG2V Bayside Hills	40.748	-73.766	20	CWOP	M	Present	NO
W2MJD Hempstead	40.712	-73.642	23	CWOP	M	Present	NO
WA2GUG New Hyde Park	40.727	-73.691	46	CWOP	M	Present	NO
WA2RSW-15 Bay Shore	40.753	-73.254	16	CWOP	M	Present	NO
WA2RSW-4 Freeport	40.750	-73.250	15	CWOP	M	Present	NO
WB2CMF Farmingville	40.837	-73.064	55	CWOP	M	Present	NO
East Moriches	40.790	-72.750	8	GPS-MET	M	Present	NO
Eastport	40.800	-72.700	30	RAWS	1/1/2004	Present	NO
Fire Island	40.617	-73.200	2	RAWS	6/1/1987	4/30/1991	NO
Long Island	40.767	-72.900	152	RAWS	10/1/2002	Present	NO
Fire Island Bay Shor	40.633	-73.267	5	SAO	M	Present	NO
Islip Long Island MacArthur AP	40.794	-73.102	26	SAO	5/1/1948	Present	NO
Moriches Lightboat S	40.783	-72.750	3	SAO	4/1/1966	Present	NO
New York City WFO	40.867	-72.867	26	SAO	7/16/1993	Present	NO
Shirley Brookhaven Airport	40.822	-72.869	25	SAO	9/29/1999	Present	NO
Westhampton Gabreski AP	40.844	-72.632	20	SAO	12/1/1942	Present	NO
Moriches East	40.783	-72.750	7	WBAN	11/1/1943	12/31/1946	NO
North Beach	40.750	-73.333	0	WBAN	M	Present	NO
Riverhead	40.867	-72.650	27	WBAN	9/1/1942	10/31/1943	NO
Tiana Long Island	40.833	-72.533	5	WBAN	10/1/1939	12/31/1944	NO
Upton	40.867	-72.883	24	WBAN	3/25/1947	9/1/1957	NO
Babylon Village Babylon	40.689	-73.333	4	WX4U	M	Present	NO
Edmunds Weather Smithtown	40.844	-73.177	15	WX4U	M	Present	NO
Floral Park	40.720	-73.700	61	WX4U	M	Present	NO
Floral Park	40.725	-73.703	30	WX4U	M	Present	NO
Levittown	40.730	-73.530	6	WX4U	M	Present	NO
Melville	40.770	-73.400	46	WX4U	M	Present	NO
Gateway National Recreational Area (GATE)							
Sandy Hook	40.463	-74.006	3	COOP	6/25/1969	Present	YES
Sandy Hook Light Stn	40.467	-74.017	5	COOP	10/1/1903	Present	YES

Name	Lat.	Lon.	Elev. (m)	Network	Start	End	In Park?
Sandy Hook	40.470	-74.010	7	GPS-MET	M	Present	YES
New York Floyd Benne	40.583	-73.883	8	SAO	12/1/1930	Present	YES
Rockaway Fort Tilden	40.567	-73.883	3	SAO	M	Present	YES
Sandy Hook Light Stn	40.467	-74.017	5	SAO	10/1/1903	Present	YES
Staten I Mlr Fld AAF	40.567	-74.100	3	WBAN	10/1/1927	12/31/1932	YES
Asbury Park	40.217	-74.017	6	COOP	11/1/1965	11/30/1978	NO
Belmar 2 SW	40.150	-74.067	12	COOP	10/1/1941	3/20/1969	NO
Bronx	40.830	-73.866	10	COOP	11/1/1894	Present	NO
Canoe Brook	40.744	-74.354	55	COOP	1/1/1931	Present	NO
Cedar Grove	40.867	-74.217	122	COOP	1/1/1941	7/3/1968	NO
Chatham	40.750	-74.367	58	COOP	2/17/1903	11/19/1965	NO
Chatham 2 W	40.744	-74.416	108	COOP	4/1/2000	2/1/2004	NO
Cranford	40.650	-74.300	23	COOP	12/1/1968	Present	NO
Elizabeth	40.667	-74.233	12	COOP	1/1/1893	2/13/1970	NO
Elizabethport	40.633	-74.200	3	COOP	8/1/1948	5/31/1964	NO
Essex Fells Serv Bld	40.831	-74.286	107	COOP	3/1/1903	Present	NO
Fort Schuyler	40.800	-73.800	18	COOP	3/1/1890	10/18/1971	NO
Freehold Marlboro	40.314	-74.251	59	COOP	1/1/1893	Present	NO
Freeport	40.667	-73.600	6	COOP	5/1/1948	11/30/1974	NO
Hackensack	40.883	-74.050	3	COOP	1/1/1953	3/31/1964	NO
Harrison	40.751	-74.157	7	COOP	6/10/1996	Present	NO
Hempstead Garden City	40.717	-73.633	24	COOP	8/1/1948	12/8/1972	NO
Hempstead Malverne	40.683	-73.667	12	COOP	1/1/1941	10/18/1966	NO
Hempstead Mitchell Fld AFB	40.733	-73.600	30	COOP	12/1/1919	4/30/1961	NO
Irvington	40.717	-74.250	27	COOP	8/1/1948	7/7/1964	NO
Jersey City	40.742	-74.057	41	COOP	12/1/1905	6/1/1997	NO
Lodi	40.867	-74.083	15	COOP	1/1/1965	4/1/1994	NO
Long Branch Oakhurst	40.280	-74.005	9	COOP	11/1/1907	Present	NO
Marlboro SCS	40.333	-74.233	37	COOP	8/1/1948	1/31/1968	NO
Mineola	40.733	-73.618	29	COOP	1/1/1938	Present	NO
Mineola 1 NE	40.749	-73.623	30	COOP	6/1/1994	1/30/2003	NO
Mineola 1 W	40.733	-73.650	27	COOP	3/1/1949	6/5/1969	NO
N Hempstead Town Doc	40.833	-73.700	0	COOP	M	5/31/1975	NO
New Brunswick 3 SE	40.472	-74.436	26	COOP	6/1/1968	Present	NO
New Brunswick Exp. Stn.	40.467	-74.433	27	COOP	1/1/1912	5/31/1968	NO
New Monmouth	40.417	-74.100	9	COOP	3/1/1961	11/30/1968	NO
New York	40.594	-73.981	6	COOP	5/1/1948	Present	NO
New York Bensonhurst	40.600	-73.967	6	COOP	1/1/1950	10/31/1953	NO
New York Botanical Gardens	40.867	-73.883	27	COOP	8/1/1973	12/31/1976	NO
New York Central Park Obs Belv	40.789	-73.967	40	COOP	1/1/1869	Present	NO
New York JFK Intl. Arpt.	40.639	-73.762	3	COOP	7/1/1948	Present	NO
New York LaGuardia Arpt.	40.779	-73.880	3	COOP	8/1/1935	Present	NO
New York Laurel Hill	40.733	-73.933	3	COOP	7/1/1950	12/31/1983	NO
New York NY Univ	40.850	-73.917	55	COOP	6/1/1939	6/7/1973	NO
New York WB City	40.700	-74.017	3	COOP	1/1/1893	1/31/1961	NO

Name	Lat.	Lon.	Elev. (m)	Network	Start	End	In Park?
New York Westerleigh	40.633	-74.117	24	COOP	5/1/1948	4/1/1992	NO
Newark	40.716	-74.176	3	COOP	3/12/1987	11/9/2000	NO
Newark Intl. Arpt.	40.683	-74.169	2	COOP	1/1/1930	Present	NO
Oceanside	40.633	-73.627	4	COOP	6/1/1994	Present	NO
Orange	40.783	-74.217	49	COOP	4/1/1940	4/28/1964	NO
Plainfield	40.604	-74.403	27	COOP	1/1/1893	Present	NO
Rahway	40.601	-74.257	6	COOP	1/1/1940	3/2/2001	NO
Ridgefield	40.833	-74.017	24	COOP	3/1/1916	6/30/1961	NO
Runyon	40.433	-74.333	6	COOP	4/1/1907	6/30/1958	NO
Rutgers Micro Met. Stn.	40.483	-74.433	40	COOP	5/1/1963	6/1/1968	NO
Rutherford	40.817	-74.117	15	COOP	3/1/1944	2/28/1952	NO
Seeley Mills	40.667	-74.400	61	COOP	11/1/1979	Present	NO
Springfield	40.696	-74.336	27	COOP	8/1/1948	3/2/2001	NO
Summit	40.717	-74.383	70	COOP	4/18/1958	1/1/1988	NO
Watchung	40.662	-74.416	79	COOP	8/1/1948	Present	NO
Westbury	40.733	-73.600	27	COOP	1/1/1980	7/1/1990	NO
Westfield	40.650	-74.350	43	COOP	11/1/1939	6/30/1961	NO
AB2NE Sayville	40.733	-73.083	6	CWOP	M	Present	NO
CW0028 Great Neck	40.807	-73.737	18	CWOP	M	Present	NO
CW0153 Floral Park	40.730	-73.705	31	CWOP	M	Present	NO
CW0205 West Islip	40.720	-73.306	11	CWOP	M	Present	NO
CW0307 Sayreville	40.457	-74.346	40	CWOP	M	Present	NO
CW0354 West Islip	40.690	-73.280	1	CWOP	M	Present	NO
CW0411 Brentwood	40.788	-73.251	124	CWOP	M	Present	NO
CW0437 Rutherford	40.823	-74.105	78	CWOP	M	Present	NO
CW0479 E. Brunswick	40.438	-74.390	41	CWOP	M	Present	NO
CW0786 Smithtown	40.848	-73.173	20	CWOP	M	Present	NO
CW0839 Colt's Neck	40.300	-74.200	23	CWOP	M	Present	NO
CW0858 Wood Ridge	40.842	-74.083	16	CWOP	M	Present	NO
CW0960 Hackensack	40.893	-74.058	22	CWOP	M	Present	NO
CW1053 Monroe Twp	40.371	-74.380	12	CWOP	M	Present	NO
CW1367 N.Middletown	40.440	-74.112	11	CWOP	M	Present	NO
CW1489 Oakland Gardens	40.740	-73.745	7	CWOP	M	Present	NO
CW1982 Lindenhurst	40.665	-73.378	2	CWOP	M	Present	NO
CW2136 Bohemia	40.763	-73.098	20	CWOP	M	Present	NO
CW2446 South River	40.445	-74.389	24	CWOP	M	Present	NO
CW2520 Babylon	40.688	-73.333	27	CWOP	M	Present	NO
CW2525 Long Beach	40.588	-73.693	3	CWOP	M	Present	NO
CW2624 New York	40.592	-73.951	4	CWOP	M	Present	NO
CW2656 Clifton	40.864	-74.170	80	CWOP	M	Present	NO
CW2685 Brooklyn	40.680	-74.001	20	CWOP	M	Present	NO
CW2963 Jersey City	40.740	-74.050	21	CWOP	M	Present	NO
CW3193 Ridgefield Park	40.856	-74.023	10	CWOP	M	Present	NO
CW3335 Bay Shore	40.741	-73.273	15	CWOP	M	Present	NO
CW3340 Valley Stream	40.651	-73.694	7	CWOP	M	Present	NO
CW3615 North Babylon	40.731	-73.324	10	CWOP	M	Present	NO

Name	Lat.	Lon.	Elev. (m)	Network	Start	End	In Park?
CW3662 Monmouth Beach	40.329	-73.976	4	CWOP	M	Present	NO
CW3712 Union	40.680	-74.234	12	CWOP	M	Present	NO
CW3877 Locust Valley	40.879	-73.592	45	CWOP	M	Present	NO
CW3942 Nutley	40.819	-74.160	17	CWOP	M	Present	NO
CW4215 Bellmore	40.676	-73.534	7	CWOP	M	Present	NO
CW4291 West New York	40.785	-74.007	150	CWOP	M	Present	NO
CW5035 Ronkonkoma	40.810	-73.123	30	CWOP	M	Present	NO
CW5086 Greenlawn	40.871	-73.352	68	CWOP	M	Present	NO
CW5425 Tenafly	40.915	-73.978	25	CWOP	M	Present	NO
CW5801 Farmingdale	40.726	-73.458	22	CWOP	M	Present	NO
CW5918 Fair Harbor	40.638	-73.184	6	CWOP	M	Present	NO
KB2JOE Brentwood	40.788	-73.252	30	CWOP	M	Present	NO
KB2KMM N. Babylon	40.743	-73.338	14	CWOP	M	Present	NO
KC2GZB Sayreville	40.458	-74.347	12	CWOP	M	Present	NO
KC2RLM-1 Chatham	40.737	-74.425	80	CWOP	M	Present	NO
KF2EO Staten Island	40.643	-74.081	58	CWOP	M	Present	NO
KF2EO-15 Staten Island	40.643	-74.081	50	CWOP	M	Present	NO
KG2V Bayside Hills	40.748	-73.766	20	CWOP	M	Present	NO
N2TNN Somerset	40.502	-74.503	5	CWOP	M	Present	NO
N9OXE Jersey City	40.720	-74.030	3	CWOP	M	Present	NO
W2MJD Hempstead	40.712	-73.642	23	CWOP	M	Present	NO
WA2GUG New Hyde Park	40.727	-73.691	46	CWOP	M	Present	NO
WA2RSW-15 Bay Shore	40.753	-73.254	16	CWOP	M	Present	NO
WA2RSW-4 Freeport	40.750	-73.250	15	CWOP	M	Present	NO
WU2Z N. Brunswick	40.450	-74.478	37	CWOP	M	Present	NO
New York	40.820	-73.950	98	GPS-MET	M	Present	NO
Union	40.680	-74.230	28	GPS-MET	M	Present	NO
Fire Island	40.617	-73.200	2	RAWS	6/1/1987	4/30/1991	NO
FRWS4 Church & Cortlandt	40.711	-74.011	24	RAWS	10/1/2001	3/31/2002	NO
FRWS5 40 River Terrace 43rd	40.718	-74.015	130	RAWS	10/1/2001	11/30/2001	NO
FRWS5 Pier 25 loading dock	40.720	-74.013	5	RAWS	11/1/2001	3/31/2002	NO
FRWS12 SW Crnr West & Vessey	40.714	-74.013	12	RAWS	10/1/2001	3/31/2002	NO
FRWS13 SE Cnr Barclay &	40.714	-74.011	12	RAWS	10/1/2001	3/31/2002	NO
FRWS14 West St. near Cedar St.	40.711	-74.015	9	RAWS	10/1/2001	3/31/2002	NO
FRWS17 Southend St Bldg 100	40.711	-74.016	12	RAWS	10/1/2001	3/31/2002	NO
Ambrose Fort Tilden	40.450	-73.817	26	SAO	M	Present	NO
Belmar Monmouth AAF	40.183	-74.117	50	SAO	1/1/1962	11/30/1963	NO
Belmar-Farmingdale Allaire AP	40.183	-74.133	48	SAO	6/1/1991	Present	NO
New York Central Park Obs Belv	40.789	-73.967	40	SAO	1/1/1869	Present	NO
New York JFK Intl. Arpt.	40.639	-73.762	3	SAO	7/1/1948	Present	NO
New York LaGuardia Arpt.	40.779	-73.880	3	SAO	8/1/1935	Present	NO

Name	Lat.	Lon.	Elev. (m)	Network	Start	End	In Park?
New York WB City	40.700	-74.017	3	SAO	1/1/1893	1/31/1961	NO
Newark Intl. Arpt.	40.683	-74.169	2	SAO	1/1/1930	Present	NO
Short Beach	40.583	-73.550	1	SAO	M	Present	NO
Teterboro Airport	40.850	-74.061	3	SAO	12/1/1946	Present	NO
Ambrose Light Stn.	40.450	-73.817	29	WBAN	11/25/1920	12/31/1987	NO
Belmar ASC	40.183	-74.067	26	WBAN	1/1/1955	8/31/1971	NO
Fort Monmouth AF	40.317	-74.033	4	WBAN	8/1/1925	12/31/1937	NO
Mineola ASC	40.700	-73.633	33	WBAN	9/1/1918	12/31/1919	NO
New York Pan Am Heli	40.750	-73.983	260	WBAN	4/1/1966	2/28/1968	NO
Red Bank AFS	40.300	-74.050	16	WBAN	12/1/1944	11/30/1948	NO
Rockaway Beach	40.567	-73.750	2	WBAN	1/1/1921	8/31/1921	NO
Babylon Village Babylon	40.689	-73.333	4	WX4U	M	Present	NO
Edmunds Weather Smithtown	40.844	-73.177	15	WX4U	M	Present	NO
Floral Park	40.720	-73.700	61	WX4U	M	Present	NO
Floral Park	40.725	-73.703	30	WX4U	M	Present	NO
Highlands	40.400	-74.000	37	WX4U	M	Present	NO
Levittown	40.730	-73.530	6	WX4U	M	Present	NO
Meadowlands Secaucus	40.796	-74.055	61	WX4U	M	Present	NO
Melville	40.770	-73.400	46	WX4U	M	Present	NO
Millburn	40.430	-74.180	7	WX4U	M	Present	NO
Piscataway	40.600	-74.400	26	WX4U	M	Present	NO
Roseland	40.820	-74.302	109	WX4U	M	Present	NO
Sands Point Shrewsbury R.	40.300	-74.000	5	WX4U	M	Present	NO
Williamsburg Brooklyn	40.718	-73.959	15	WX4U	M	Present	NO
Sagamore Hill National Historic Site (SAHI)							
Babylon	40.717	-73.367	15	COOP	3/1/1918	11/30/1974	NO
Brentwood	40.783	-73.250	31	COOP	1/1/1893	8/1/1976	NO
Bronx	40.830	-73.866	10	COOP	11/1/1894	Present	NO
Centerport	40.884	-73.372	9	COOP	10/18/2001	Present	NO
Dix Hills	40.800	-73.300	37	COOP	11/1/1987	10/31/1991	NO
Eastchester	40.933	-73.800	37	COOP	6/15/1944	11/30/1974	NO
Farmingdale 2 NE	40.750	-73.433	24	COOP	12/1/1916	12/31/1956	NO
Fire Island	40.633	-73.267	9	COOP	10/1/1939	Present	NO
Fort Schuyler	40.800	-73.800	18	COOP	3/1/1890	10/18/1971	NO
Freeport	40.667	-73.600	6	COOP	5/1/1948	11/30/1974	NO
Hempstead Garden City	40.717	-73.633	24	COOP	8/1/1948	12/8/1972	NO
Hempstead Malverne	40.683	-73.667	12	COOP	1/1/1941	10/18/1966	NO
Hempstead Mitchell Fld AFB	40.733	-73.600	30	COOP	12/1/1919	4/30/1961	NO
Holbrook	40.833	-73.083	24	COOP	3/16/1972	12/31/1979	NO
Islip Long Island MacArthur AP	40.794	-73.102	26	COOP	5/1/1948	Present	NO
Lake Ronkonkoma	40.833	-73.133	24	COOP	5/1/1948	3/16/1972	NO
Larchmont	40.933	-73.750	12	COOP	5/1/1948	Present	NO
Mineola	40.733	-73.618	29	COOP	1/1/1938	Present	NO
Mineola 1 NE	40.749	-73.623	30	COOP	6/1/1994	1/30/2003	NO

Name	Lat.	Lon.	Elev. (m)	Network	Start	End	In Park?
Mineola 1 W	40.733	-73.650	27	COOP	3/1/1949	6/5/1969	NO
N Hempstead Town Doc	40.833	-73.700	0	COOP	M	5/31/1975	NO
New York Botanical Gardens	40.867	-73.883	27	COOP	8/1/1973	12/31/1976	NO
New York Central Park Obs Belv	40.789	-73.967	40	COOP	1/1/1869	Present	NO
New York JFK Intl. Arpt.	40.639	-73.762	3	COOP	7/1/1948	Present	NO
New York LaGuardia Arpt.	40.779	-73.880	3	COOP	8/1/1935	Present	NO
New York Laurel Hill	40.733	-73.933	3	COOP	7/1/1950	12/31/1983	NO
New York NY Univ	40.850	-73.917	55	COOP	6/1/1939	6/7/1973	NO
Northport	40.900	-73.350	6	COOP	1/1/1942	9/30/1953	NO
Oceanside	40.633	-73.627	4	COOP	6/1/1994	Present	NO
Patchogue 2 N	40.797	-73.001	17	COOP	5/1/1937	11/1/1997	NO
Port Jefferson	40.950	-73.067	3	COOP	11/1/1952	7/31/1976	NO
Sayville Solar Rad	40.767	-73.083	18	COOP	7/1/1952	Present	NO
Sea Cliff	40.851	-73.648	30	COOP	9/1/1994	Present	NO
Setauket 2	40.950	-73.100	12	COOP	M	12/31/1975	NO
Setauket Strong	40.959	-73.105	12	COOP	8/1/1885	Present	NO
Vanderbilt Museum	40.900	-73.367	34	COOP	4/1/1976	6/12/1991	NO
Wantagh Cedar Creek	40.655	-73.505	3	COOP	7/1/1975	Present	NO
Westbury	40.733	-73.600	27	COOP	1/1/1980	7/1/1990	NO
AB2NE Sayville	40.733	-73.083	6	CWOP	M	Present	NO
CW0028 Great Neck	40.807	-73.737	18	CWOP	M	Present	NO
CW0153 Floral Park	40.730	-73.705	31	CWOP	M	Present	NO
CW0205 West Islip	40.720	-73.306	11	CWOP	M	Present	NO
CW0354 West Islip	40.690	-73.280	1	CWOP	M	Present	NO
CW0411 Brentwood	40.788	-73.251	124	CWOP	M	Present	NO
CW0461 Mt.Sinai	40.940	-73.037	45	CWOP	M	Present	NO
CW0786 Smithtown	40.848	-73.173	20	CWOP	M	Present	NO
CW1489 Oakland Gardens	40.740	-73.745	7	CWOP	M	Present	NO
CW1982 Lindenhurst	40.665	-73.378	2	CWOP	M	Present	NO
CW2136 Bohemia	40.763	-73.098	20	CWOP	M	Present	NO
CW2520 Babylon	40.688	-73.333	27	CWOP	M	Present	NO
CW2525 Long Beach	40.588	-73.693	3	CWOP	M	Present	NO
CW3335 Bay Shore	40.741	-73.273	15	CWOP	M	Present	NO
CW3340 Valley Stream	40.651	-73.694	7	CWOP	M	Present	NO
CW3615 North Babylon	40.731	-73.324	10	CWOP	M	Present	NO
CW3877 Locust Valley	40.879	-73.592	45	CWOP	M	Present	NO
CW4215 Bellmore	40.676	-73.534	7	CWOP	M	Present	NO
CW5035 Ronkonkoma	40.810	-73.123	30	CWOP	M	Present	NO
CW5086 Greenlawn	40.871	-73.352	68	CWOP	M	Present	NO
CW5202 Mount Sinai	40.925	-73.017	49	CWOP	M	Present	NO
CW5425 Tenafly	40.915	-73.978	25	CWOP	M	Present	NO
CW5801 Farmingdale	40.726	-73.458	22	CWOP	M	Present	NO
CW5918 Fair Harbor	40.638	-73.184	6	CWOP	M	Present	NO
KB2JOE Brentwood	40.788	-73.252	30	CWOP	M	Present	NO
KB2KMM N. Babylon	40.743	-73.338	14	CWOP	M	Present	NO

Name	Lat.	Lon.	Elev. (m)	Network	Start	End	In Park?
KC2KY Centereach	40.872	-73.088	31	CWOP	M	Present	NO
KD1F Farmingville	40.839	-73.060	60	CWOP	M	Present	NO
KG2V Bayside Hills	40.748	-73.766	20	CWOP	M	Present	NO
W2MJD Hempstead	40.712	-73.642	23	CWOP	M	Present	NO
WA2GUG New Hyde Park	40.727	-73.691	46	CWOP	M	Present	NO
WA2RSW-15 Bay Shore	40.753	-73.254	16	CWOP	M	Present	NO
WA2RSW-4 Freeport	40.750	-73.250	15	CWOP	M	Present	NO
WB2CMF Farmingville	40.837	-73.064	55	CWOP	M	Present	NO
New York	40.820	-73.950	98	GPS-MET	M	Present	NO
Fire Island	40.617	-73.200	2	RAWS	6/1/1987	4/30/1991	NO
Eaton's Neck Light Stn.	40.950	-73.400	15	SAO	12/1/1958	Present	NO
Execution Rock Light	40.883	-73.733	8	SAO	5/1/1968	Present	NO
Farmingdale Republic AP	40.734	-73.417	25	SAO	11/1/1954	Present	NO
Fire Island Bay Shor	40.633	-73.267	5	SAO	M	Present	NO
Islip Long Island MacArthur AP	40.794	-73.102	26	SAO	5/1/1948	Present	NO
New York Central Park Obs Belv	40.789	-73.967	40	SAO	1/1/1869	Present	NO
New York JFK Intl. Arpt.	40.639	-73.762	3	SAO	7/1/1948	Present	NO
New York LaGuardia Arpt.	40.779	-73.880	3	SAO	8/1/1935	Present	NO
Short Beach	40.583	-73.550	1	SAO	M	Present	NO
Farmingdale AAF	40.733	-73.400	19	WBAN	4/1/1943	12/31/1943	NO
Mineola ASC	40.700	-73.633	33	WBAN	9/1/1918	12/31/1919	NO
North Beach	40.750	-73.333	0	WBAN	M	Present	NO
Rockaway Beach	40.567	-73.750	2	WBAN	1/1/1921	8/31/1921	NO
Babylon Village Babylon	40.689	-73.333	4	WX4U	M	Present	NO
Edmunds Weather Smithtown	40.844	-73.177	15	WX4U	M	Present	NO
Floral Park	40.725	-73.703	30	WX4U	M	Present	NO
Floral Park	40.720	-73.700	61	WX4U	M	Present	NO
Levittown	40.730	-73.530	6	WX4U	M	Present	NO
Melville	40.770	-73.400	46	WX4U	M	Present	NO

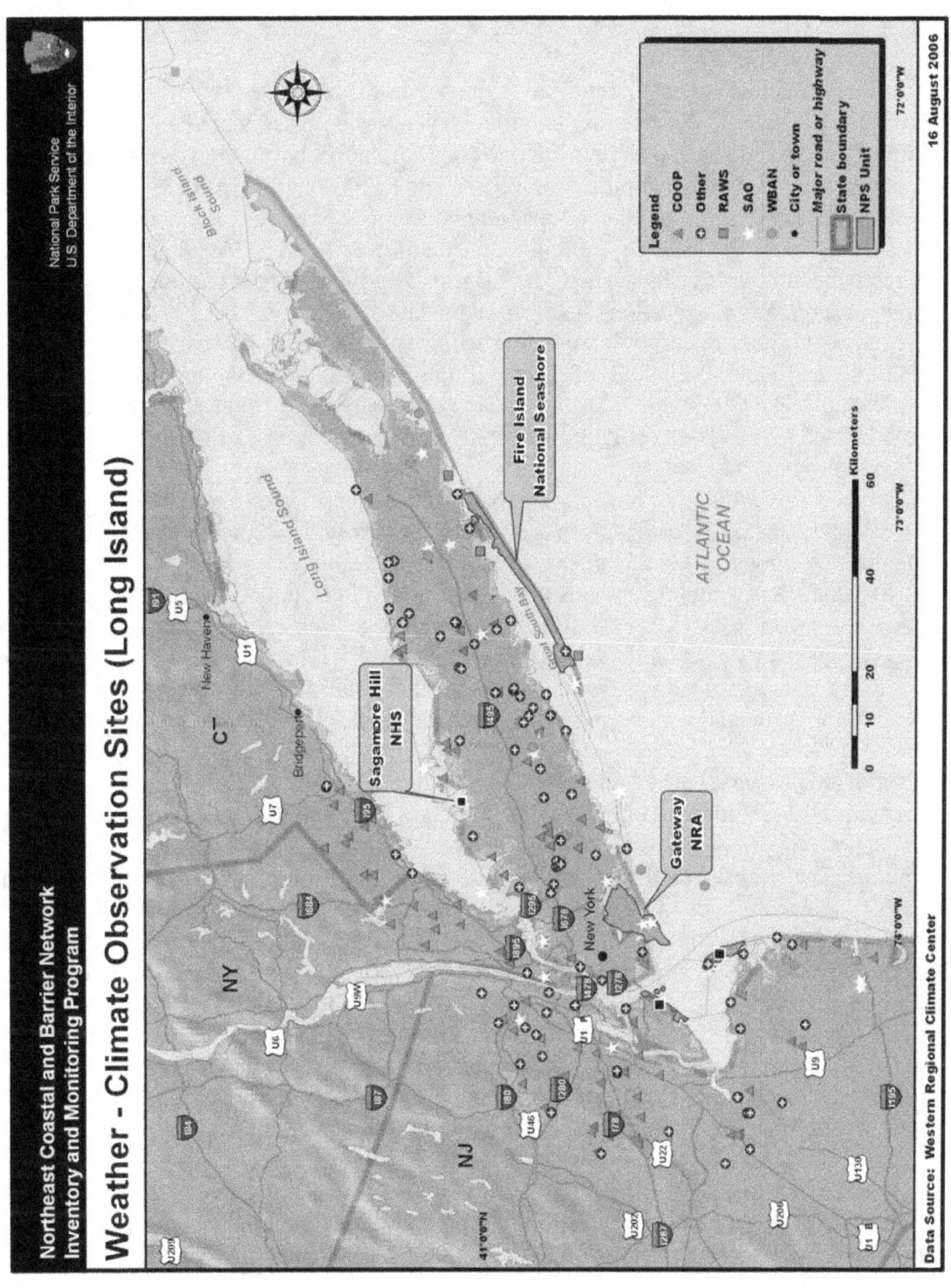

Figure 4.2. Station locations for NCBN park units on Long Island, New York.

39

4.2.3. Greater Chesapeake Bay Region Park Units

The coverage of weather/climate stations in or near NCBN park units in the greater Chesapeake Bay region is quite dense. Assateague Island National Seashore (ASIS) is the only park unit in this region having weather/climate stations inside its park boundaries; the rest of the park units have no stations inside park boundaries (Table 4.5; Figure 4.3). The park unit having the least station coverage is GEWA.

There are four stations that we have identified within ASIS (Table 4.5). Two of these are active, including the COOP station "Assateague" and the RAWS station "Assateague Island". The COOP station "Assateague" has operated since 1968. There are occasional gaps one month or longer in length throughout the station's data record. The RAWS station in ASIS has been operating since the early 1990s and is well-maintained by ASIS staff (Conner and Albert 2004). The longest climate records for ASIS are found outside of the park. The COOP station "Ocean City" has been operating since 1898. The COOP station "Snow Hill 4 N" has operated since 1916; with the exception of a year-long data gap in the late 1960s, this record is largely complete. Four SAO sites are currently operating within 30 km of ASIS. Most of these stations are located at the north and south sides of ASIS. Of these SAO stations, the longest period of record is found at Ocean City, which starting making observations in 1898. A POMS station (Assateague Island NS) has been operating since 2005 just outside the northwest edge of ASIS.

In addition to the above stations, Conner and Albert (2004) identified two rain gauges at the ASIS visitor center. One of the rain gauges is maintained to provide visitor information about current weather conditions, while the other provides backup rainfall data for the other stations within ASIS. Conner and Albert (2004) also identified a NADP station, "Assateague Island National Seashore-Woodcock (MD18)". Information on this station can be found at http://nadp.sws.uiuc.edu/sites/siteinfo.asp?net=NTN&id=MD18. However, at the time this report was prepared, we were unable to verify data access for these stations (see Appendix H), so they are not listed in the main stations lists provided in this chapter.

Colonial National Historical Park (COLO) has no weather/climate stations located inside its boundaries (Table 4.5). Within 30 km of COLO, there are four active COOP stations, one active GPS-MET station, six active SAO stations, one active WX4U station, and at least ten active CWOP stations. The closest COOP station to COLO is "Williamsburg 2 N", whose data record goes back to 1948 and has a complete data record. The closest SAO station to COLO is "Williamsburg Jamestown Arpt.", a station that has only been operating since 2003. The stations with the longest periods of record are the COOP and SAO stations at Langley Air Force Base (Langley AFB), about 20 km southeast of COLO (Figure 4.3). Both of these stations have records extending back to 1893. The COOP station at Langely AFB has occasional gaps of up to a few months in length, breaking up the otherwise complete data record. Conner and Albert (2004) identified an automated weather station at the Virginia Chesapeake National Estuarine Research Reserve (Appendix H), which could provide useful weather and climate data for COLO.

We have identified no weather/climate stations within GEWA. Although temperature and precipitation have been measured at the GEWA visitor center (Conner and Albert 2004; see

Appendix H), it is not clear whether there is an official weather station at this site and how to obtain data from these instruments. The only active COOP stations within 30 km are "Mechanicsville 5 NE", about 30 km northeast of GEWA, and "Warsaw 2 NW", about 20 km southeast of GEWA (Table 4.5). The COOP station "Mechanicsville 5 NE" has been active since 1927 but has an unreliable data record. The COOP station "Warsaw 2 NW" has a very reliable data record that starts in 1893. The only other active stations around GEWA are seven CWOP stations.

Thomas Stone National Historic Site (THST) has no stations within its boundaries. Despite the proximity of THST to the southern side of the Washington, D.C. metropolitan area, only two COOP stations and two SAO stations are currently active within 30 km of THST (Table 4.5). The active COOP stations include the aforementioned station "Mechanicsville 5 NE" and the "Oxon Hill" COOP station, which has operated since 1994. Due to the lack of reliable data from "Mechanicsville 5 NE", the most reliable long-term records for the THST vicinity are found at the two active SAO stations, "Davison AAF" and "Quantico MCAS". The latter station has been active since 1922 and has a reliable data record, while the former station has been operating since 1957. There are at least a dozen CWOP stations providing real-time weather data in the vicinity of THST.

Table 4.5. Weather/climate stations for NCBN park units in the greater Chesapeake Bay region. Stations inside park units and within 30 km of the park unit boundary are included. Missing entries are indicated by "M".

Name	Lat.	Lon.	Elev. (m)	Network	Start	End	In Park?
Assateague Island National Seashore (ASIS)							
Assateague	38.072	-75.213	3	COOP	7/1/1968	Present	YES
Chincoteague Wildlife	37.917	-75.350	3	COOP	8/1/1961	7/31/1973	YES
Assateague Island	38.067	-75.201	4	RAWS	5/1/1993	Present	YES
Assateague Beach	37.867	-75.367	6	WBAN	7/1/1939	12/31/1946	YES
Berlin 2 NE	38.350	-75.200	6	COOP	6/1/1899	2/28/1954	NO
Camp Barnes 1 SE	38.500	-75.083	3	COOP	M	Present	NO
Chincoteague NAS	37.933	-75.467	12	COOP	11/1/1948	2/12/1959	NO
Indian River Stn.	38.617	-75.067	2	COOP	9/1/1955	4/30/1974	NO
Ocean City	38.333	-75.083	6	COOP	4/1/1898	Present	NO
Ocean City Motel	38.350	-75.083	6	COOP	M	7/30/1968	NO
Pocomoke City	38.067	-75.550	6	COOP	4/1/1894	9/30/1979	NO
Rehoboth Beach LBS	38.617	-75.067	3	COOP	M	Present	NO
Selbyville	38.467	-75.217	9	COOP	1/1/1954	8/1/1970	NO
Snow Hill 4 N	38.236	-75.379	9	COOP	3/1/1916	Present	NO
Wallops Island Wallops Flight	37.941	-75.463	12	COOP	11/21/1961	Present	NO
Whaleysville	38.400	-75.300	9	COOP	12/1/1948	8/31/1951	NO
Assateague Island NS	38.251	-75.159	3	POMS	6/16/2005	Present	NO
Chincoteague	37.933	-75.350	2	RAWS	3/1/1997	Present	NO
Powellville	38.350	-75.417	5	RAWS	12/1/2004	Present	NO
Indian River Stn.	38.617	-75.067	2	SAO	9/1/1955	Present	NO
Ocean City	38.333	-75.083	6	SAO	4/1/1898	Present	NO

Name	Lat.	Lon.	Elev. (m)	Network	Start	End	In Park?
Ocean City Municipal AP	38.308	-75.124	4	SAO	9/1/1999	Present	NO
Wallops Island Wallops Flight	37.941	-75.463	12	SAO	11/21/1961	Present	NO
Wallops Station Upper Air Unit	37.850	-75.483	3	SAO	3/1/1960	6/1/1984	NO
Chincoteague NAS	37.933	-75.433	15	WBAN	3/1/1943	3/31/1959	NO
Snow Hill	38.183	-75.400	8	WBAN	1/1/1938	12/31/1948	NO

Colonial National Historical Park (COLO)

Name	Lat.	Lon.	Elev. (m)	Network	Start	End	In Park?
Cardinal	37.417	-76.367	3	COOP	8/1/1947	8/31/1950	NO
Dendron 1 SW	37.033	-76.950	18	COOP	12/7/1957	1/8/1960	NO
Glenns 1 S	37.550	-76.617	34	COOP	6/1/1951	12/31/1952	NO
Hampton University	37.023	-76.337	3	COOP	11/10/2002	Present	NO
Langley AFB	37.083	-76.350	6	COOP	3/3/1893	Present	NO
Mathews 4 SE	37.403	-76.269	2	COOP	8/1/1950	3/31/2000	NO
Newport News Press B	37.017	-76.450	15	COOP	11/1/1898	12/31/1980	NO
North	37.434	-76.441	3	COOP	4/1/2000	Present	NO
Smithfield	36.983	-76.633	12	COOP	5/17/1941	2/28/1975	NO
Surry 4 SW	37.083	-76.867	37	COOP	6/1/1941	3/1/1955	NO
Wakefield 1 NW	37.000	-77.000	31	COOP	1/1/1960	7/31/1978	NO
Williamsburg 2 N	37.302	-76.704	21	COOP	8/1/1948	Present	NO
Williamsburg 2 NW	37.283	-76.750	31	COOP	10/1/1896	5/31/1951	NO
CW0947 Yorktown	37.169	-76.471	32	CWOP	M	Present	NO
CW1566 Gloucester	37.551	-76.529	5	CWOP	M	Present	NO
CW2394 Smithfield	36.994	-76.601	19	CWOP	M	Present	NO
CW3777 Hampton	37.089	-76.421	3	CWOP	M	Present	NO
CW3801 Hampton	37.070	-76.320	10	CWOP	M	Present	NO
CW5207 Williamsburg	37.317	-76.750	5	CWOP	M	Present	NO
CW5473 Hampton	37.048	-76.300	3	CWOP	M	Present	NO
KD7PJQ-2 Hampton	37.063	-76.326	3	CWOP	M	Present	NO
KF4HJW Tide	37.100	-76.545	7	CWOP	M	Present	NO
W4FLS Newport News	37.072	-76.486	8	CWOP	M	Present	NO
WC4R Williamsburg	37.247	-76.652	8	CWOP	M	Present	NO
Driver	36.960	-76.560	13	GPS-MET	M	Present	NO
Fort Eustis Felker AAF	37.133	-76.600	7	SAO	11/1/1960	Present	NO
Langley AFB	37.083	-76.350	6	SAO	3/3/1893	Present	NO
Middle Peninsula Regional Arpt.	37.521	-76.765	7	SAO	1/7/2004	Present	NO
Milford Haven	37.483	-76.317	3	SAO	11/1/1971	Present	NO
Newport News Intl. Arpt.	37.132	-76.493	13	SAO	11/1/1949	Present	NO
Williamsburg Jamestown Airport	37.239	-76.716	15	SAO	4/23/2003	Present	NO
Fort Eustis ASC	37.133	-76.600	11	WBAN	11/1/1920	12/31/1930	NO
Newport News	37.074	-76.500	9	WX4U	M	Present	NO

George Washington Birthplace National Monument (GEWA)

Name	Lat.	Lon.	Elev. (m)	Network	Start	End	In Park?
Charlotte Hall	38.467	-76.750	52	COOP	6/1/1893	6/16/1961	NO
Charlotte Hall 2 SE	38.467	-76.767	51	COOP	7/1/1961	1/1/1973	NO

Name	Lat.	Lon.	Elev. (m)	Network	Start	End	In Park?
Colonial Beach	38.251	-76.963	3	COOP	12/1/1963	10/21/2002	NO
Dahlgren	38.317	-77.033	21	COOP	11/8/1961	8/26/1998	NO
Dahlgren Weapons Lab	38.333	-77.033	6	COOP	5/1/1920	12/31/1963	NO
La Plata 1 W	38.533	-77.000	43	COOP	12/1/1894	10/1/1998	NO
Leonardtown 2	38.300	-76.650	31	COOP	10/1/1949	3/31/1950	NO
Leonardtown 3 NW	38.317	-76.667	34	COOP	8/1/1959	3/31/1976	NO
Leonardtown 4 SSW	38.250	-76.650	6	COOP	1/1/1893	8/31/1959	NO
Mechanicsville	38.450	-76.733	52	COOP	9/1/1927	2/28/1935	NO
Mechanicsville 5 NE	38.462	-76.699	30	COOP	7/10/1927	Present	NO
Tall Timbers	38.167	-76.550	4	COOP	5/1/1988	1/1/1991	NO
Warsaw 2 NW	37.988	-76.777	43	COOP	1/1/1893	Present	NO
CW1387 Hughesville	38.518	-76.764	20	CWOP	M	Present	NO
CW2816 Port Royal	38.166	-77.195	16	CWOP	M	Present	NO
CW3754 Leonardtown	38.351	-76.625	39	CWOP	M	Present	NO
CW5125 Newburg	38.319	-76.927	2	CWOP	M	Present	NO
KI4GKE Port Royal	38.166	-77.195	17	CWOP	M	Present	NO
W3SMR-8 Golden Beach	38.494	-76.702	27	CWOP	M	Present	NO
WX3SMD-8 Mechanicsville	38.494	-76.702	20	CWOP	M	Present	NO
Dahlgren	38.317	-77.033	21	SAO	11/8/1961	8/26/1998	NO
Thomas Stone National Historic Site (THST)							
Alexandria City Garage	38.800	-77.083	21	COOP	2/1/1958	10/1/1975	NO
Alexandria Potomac Y	38.817	-77.050	6	COOP	4/1/1893	10/31/1962	NO
Charlotte Hall	38.467	-76.750	52	COOP	6/1/1893	6/16/1961	NO
Charlotte Hall 2 SE	38.467	-76.767	51	COOP	7/1/1961	1/1/1973	NO
Cheltenham 1 NW	38.733	-76.850	70	COOP	5/1/1901	10/31/1956	NO
Colonial Beach	38.251	-76.963	3	COOP	12/1/1963	10/21/2002	NO
Dahlgren	38.317	-77.033	21	COOP	11/8/1961	8/26/1998	NO
Dahlgren Weapons Lab	38.333	-77.033	6	COOP	5/1/1920	12/31/1963	NO
Episcopal High School	38.817	-77.100	76	COOP	10/1/1945	2/28/1958	NO
Ft. Washington NP	38.717	-77.033	37	COOP	6/1/1968	8/31/1975	NO
Groveton	38.767	-77.100	76	COOP	11/1/1951	1/1/1973	NO
Indianhead	38.592	-77.158	11	COOP	1/23/1998	3/31/1998	NO
La Plata 1 W	38.533	-77.000	43	COOP	12/1/1894	10/1/1998	NO
Leonardtown 3 NW	38.317	-76.667	34	COOP	8/1/1959	3/31/1976	NO
Mason Springs	38.583	-77.100	9	COOP	10/1/1994	2/1/1998	NO
Mechanicsville	38.450	-76.733	52	COOP	9/1/1927	2/28/1935	NO
Mechanicsville 5 NE	38.462	-76.699	30	COOP	7/10/1927	Present	NO
Oxon Hill	38.796	-76.995	37	COOP	5/1/1994	Present	NO
Quantico 1 S	38.500	-77.317	3	COOP	4/1/1896	3/31/1976	NO
Waldorf 4 W	38.642	-76.986	64	COOP	7/1/1994	10/26/2002	NO
Waldorf Police Barrack	38.652	-76.881	64	COOP	8/1/1948	1/4/2002	NO
CW0980 Springfield	38.739	-77.238	211	CWOP	M	Present	NO
CW1167 Fort Belvoir	38.710	-77.192	120	CWOP	M	Present	NO
CW1387 Hughesville	38.518	-76.764	20	CWOP	M	Present	NO
CW2579 Accokeek	38.667	-77.037	81	CWOP	M	Present	NO
CW3438 Hollis Point	38.635	-77.110	10	CWOP	M	Present	NO

Name	Lat.	Lon.	Elev. (m)	Network	Start	End	In Park?
CW3754 Leonardtown	38.351	-76.625	39	CWOP	M	Present	NO
CW5125 Newburg	38.319	-76.927	2	CWOP	M	Present	NO
CW5127 Alexandria	38.796	-77.121	55	CWOP	M	Present	NO
CW5223 Lorton	38.717	-77.201	28	CWOP	M	Present	NO
K3GJ-1 La Plata	38.580	-76.996	64	CWOP	M	Present	NO
K3WTF Potomac Hts.	38.605	-77.136	25	CWOP	M	Present	NO
KA5TUU Alexandria	38.810	-77.093	77	CWOP	M	Present	NO
KA6AKH Alexandria	38.728	-77.046	16	CWOP	M	Present	NO
W3SMR-8 Golden Beach	38.494	-76.702	27	CWOP	M	Present	NO
WX3SMD-8 Mechanicsville	38.494	-76.702	20	CWOP	M	Present	NO
Cedarville	38.653	-76.821	61	RAWS	12/1/2004	Present	NO
Dahlgren	38.317	-77.033	21	SAO	11/8/1961	8/26/1998	NO
Davison AAF	38.717	-77.183	27	SAO	2/1/1957	Present	NO
Quantico MCAS	38.500	-77.300	4	SAO	9/1/1922	Present	NO
Upper Marlboro	38.751	-76.820	61	WX4U	M	Present	NO

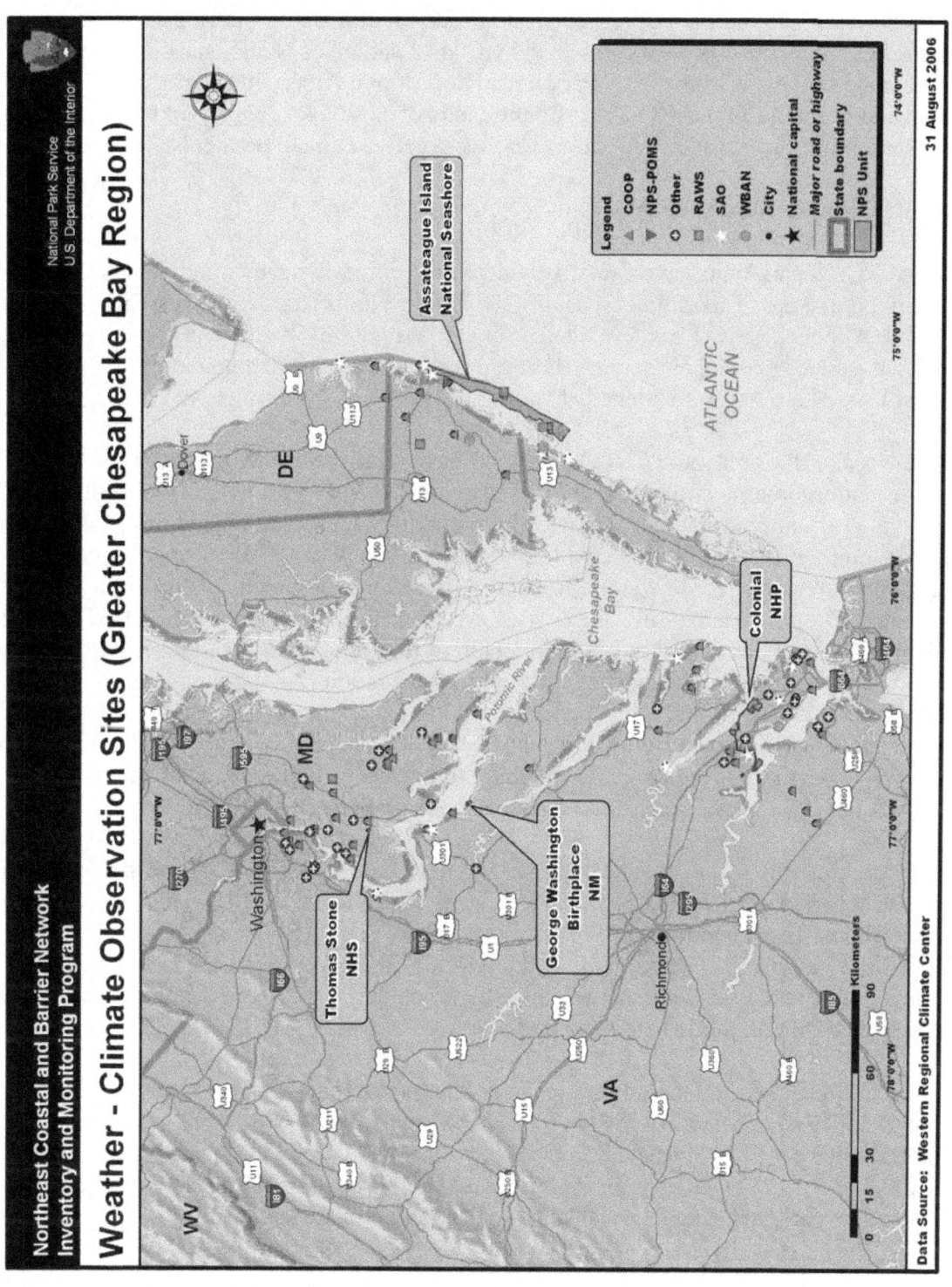

Figure 4.3. Station locations for NCBN park units in the greater Chesapeake Bay region.

5.0. Conclusions and Recommendations

We have based our findings on an examination of the presently-available weather/climate station metadata and data records in and near NCBN park units, discussions with NPS staff and other collaborators, and prior knowledge of the area. Here, we offer an evaluation and general comments pertaining to the status, prospects, and needs for climate-monitoring capabilities in the NCBN. Preliminary work has been completed by CACO and other NCBN staff to identify weather/climate stations within NCBN park units (Conner and Albert 2004), particularly those stations in and near CACO (CACO 2001; Conner and Albert 2004). This report builds on these previous station inventories and suggestions for investigative climate protocols.

5.1. NCBN Climate Monitoring Status

Most of the NCBN park units have a relatively dense coverage of weather and climate stations in or near park boundaries. This is true especially for the park units near New York City and on Long Island. Although CACO has few weather or climate stations in areas surrounding it, due to its somewhat isolated geographic setting, there are several manual and automatic stations that are either in or very near CACO, positioned at various useful locations throughout CACO.

In the Chesapeake Bay area, both COLO and ASIS have relatively dense coverages of weather and climate stations in or near the park units. However, two other park units, GEWA and THST, currently have very limited station coverage within 30 km of their park boundaries. There is only one reliable long-term record available within 30 km of GEWA, while the primary source of automated measurements for GEWA are from CWOP stations for which data reliability is not always certain. Despite its proximity to the Washington, D.C. metropolitan area, THST has only two reliable long-term climate records within 30 km of its boundaries. These records come from SAO stations, which are also the most reliable automated stations for this area. Due to the limited number of active stations for these two parks, the continued operation of those COOP and SAO stations with long-term climate records is critically important. Active partnerships between NPS and the NWS offices in this region can help ensure that these valuable stations remain active and provide useful data for NPS research and management activities.

These partnerships will also insure the continued operation of several COOP and SAO stations in or near NCBN park units that currently provide extremely valuable long-term data records going back to the 1800s. These include the "Provincetown 3 NW" in CACO, the COOP and SAO stations at New York City's Central Park, and the COOP and SAO stations at Langley AFB. These longer climate records are generally more common in the NCBN and other areas in the eastern U.S. than they are elsewhere in the U.S.

At the present time, metadata records are severely lacking for many of the local NPS weather and climate stations identified by CACO (2001) and Conner and Albert (2004). These stations are listed in Appendix H. Basic metadata such as latitude and longitude, elevation, and station period of record were not available for most of these stations. We therefore encourage continued efforts to collect such metadata for local NPS weather and climate stations.

5.2. Spatial Variations in Mean Climate

If only a few stations will be installed in a region, the primary goal should be to define the overall characteristics of the main climate elements (temperature and precipitation and their joint relative, snow) in that region. Once this objective is met, additional stations would be best used for two important and somewhat competing purposes (see Appendix B): (a) add redundancy as backup for loss of data from current stations (or loss of the physical stations) or (b) provide added information on spatial heterogeneity in climate arising from topographic diversity.

5.3. Climate Change Detection

The need for credible, accurate, complete, and long-term climate records—from any location—cannot be overemphasized in a climate monitoring program. This is particularly relevant for the monitoring of climate change. When choosing a station for inclusion in a long-term climate monitoring program, several factors must be considered, as summarized in Appendix B. The data records from these stations should cover several decades or more in order to be able to depict those climate variations that occur at longer temporal scales. The data records should be very complete, with few if any gaps. The measurements from these stations should, of course, be accurate; this can be checked by cross-referencing with measurements from any nearby stations. The best stations for long-term monitoring programs are those stations that have relatively few, if any, changes in the station characteristics over time. These changes include station moves, instrumentation changes, variations in the observation time, observer changes, etc.

The need for long-term climate records that are complete and of high quality is always a top priority in any climate monitoring program. However, because of spatial diversity in climate, monitoring that fills knowledge gaps and provides information on long-term temporal variability in short-distance relationships is also valuable. We cannot be sure that climate variability and climate change will affect all parts of a given park unit equally. In fact, it is appropriate to speculate that this is not the case, and spatial variations in temporal variability can extend to small spatial scales (a few kilometers or less in some cases).

5.4. Aesthetics

This issue arises frequently enough to deserve comment. Standards for quality climate measurements require open exposures away from heat sources, buildings, pavement, close vegetation and tall trees, and human intrusion (thus away from property lines). By their nature, sites that meet these standards are usually quite visible. In many settings (such as heavily forested areas) these sites also are quite rare, making them precisely the same places that managers wish to protect from aesthetic intrusion. The most suitable and scientifically defensible sites frequently are rejected as candidate locations for weather/climate stations. Most weather/climate stations, therefore, tend to be "hidden" but many of these hidden locations have inferior exposures. Some measure of compromise is nearly always called for in siting weather and climate stations.

The public has vast interest and curiosity in weather and climate, and within the NPS I&M networks, such measurements consistently rate near or at the top of desired public information.

47

There seem to be many possible opportunities for exploiting and embracing this widespread interest within the interpretive mission of the NPS. One way to do this would be to highlight rather than hide these stations and educate the public about the need for adequate siting. We have encountered a number of weather stations within NPS park units that have served inadvertently as examples for how measurements should not be made.

5.5. Information Access

Access to information promotes its use, which in turn promotes attention to station care and maintenance, better data, and more use. An end-to-end view that extends from sensing to decision support is far preferable to isolated and disconnected activities and aids the support infrastructure that is ultimately so necessary for successful, long-term climate monitoring.

Decisions about improvements in monitoring capacity are facilitated greatly by the ability to examine available climate information. Various methods are being created at WRCC to improve access to that information. Web pages providing historic and ongoing climate data, and information from NCBN park units can be accessed at http://www.wrcc.dri.edu/nps. In the event that this URL changes, there still will be links from the main WRCC Web page entitled "Projects" under NPS.

The WRCC has been steadily developing software to summarize data from hourly sites. This has been occurring under the aegis of the RAWS program and a growing array of product generators ranging from daily and monthly data lists to wind roses and hourly frequency distributions. All park data are available to park personnel via an access code (needed only for data listings) that can be acquired by request. The WRCC RAWS Web page is located at http://www.wrcc.dri.edu/wraws or http://www.raws.dri.edu.

Web pages have been developed to provide access not only to historic and ongoing climate data and information from NCBN park units but also to climate-monitoring efforts for NCBN. These pages can be found through http://www.wrcc.dri.edu/nps.

Additional access to more standard climate information is accessible though the previously mentioned Web pages, as well as through http://www.wrcc.dri.edu/summary. These summaries are generally for COOP stations.

5.6. Summarized Conclusions and Recommendations

- Preliminary work has been done by the NCBN to locate weather/climate stations. Much of this initial work has focused on climate monitoring efforts around CACO.
- Most of the NCBN park units have satisfactorily dense weather/climate station coverage within 30 km of the park units. This is particularly true for NCBN park units on Long Island and near New York City.
- Weather/climate station coverage and access to long-term climate records is quite limited for GEWA and THST, in the Chesapeake Bay region. It is therefore critically important to retain any existing longer-term climate stations in the area.

- At the present time, metadata for local NPS stations inside NCBN park units is largely incomplete. Fundamental information such as station location coordinates and period of record is largely missing for these local stations.

6.0. Literature Cited

American Association of State Climatologists. 1985. Heights and exposure standards for sensors on automated weather stations. The State Climatologist **9**.

Aubrey, D. G. and P. E. Speer. 1985. A study of non-linear tidal propagation in shallow inlet/estuarine systems. Part I: observations. Estuarine, Coastal and Shelf Science **21**:185-205.

Bevis, M., S. Businger, T. A. Herring, C. Rocken, R. A. Anthes, and R. H. Ware. 1992. GPS meteorology: remote sensing of the atmospheric water vapor using the global positioning system. Journal of Geophysical Research **97**:75–94.

Bonan, G. B. 2002. Ecological Climatology: Concepts and Applications. Cambridge University Press.

Bureau of Land Management. 1997. Remote Automatic Weather Station (RAWS) and Remote Environmental Monitoring Systems (REMS) standards. RAWS/REMS Support Facility, Boise, Idaho.

Cape Cod National Seashore (CACO). 2001. Summary of meteorologic and atmospheric monitoring protocols for Cape Cod National Seashore. Online. (http://www.nature.nps.gov/im/monitor/protocoldb.cfm). Accessed 30 April 2006.

Chapin III, F. S., M. S. Torn, and M. Tateno. 1996. Principles of ecosystem sustainability. The American Naturalist **148**:1016-1037.

Conner, C., and M. Albert. 2004. Weather station inventory and preliminary needs assessment for the Northeast Coastal and Barrier Network. National Park Service. Boston, Massachusetts.

Culliton, T. J., M. A. Warren, T. R. Goodspeed, D. G. Remer C. M. Blackwell, and J. J. McDonough III. 1990. Fifty years of population change along the nation's coasts, 1960-2010. National Oceanic and Atmospheric Administration, Strategic Assessment Branch, Rockville, Maryland.

Daly, C., R. P. Neilson, and D. L. Phillips. 1994. A statistical-topographic model for mapping climatological precipitation over mountainous terrain. Journal of Applied Meteorology **33**:140-158.

Daly, C., W. P. Gibson, G. H. Taylor, G. L. Johnson, and P. Pasteris. 2002. A knowledge-based approach to the statistical mapping of climate. Climate Research **22**:99-113.

Doggett, M., C. Daly, J. Smith, W. Gibson, G. Taylor, G. Johnson, and P. Pasteris. 2004. High-resolution 1971-2000 mean monthly temperature maps for the western United States. Fourteenth AMS Conf. on Applied Climatology, 84th AMS Annual Meeting. Seattle,

Washington, American Meteorological Society, Boston, Massachusetts, January 2004, Paper 4.3, CD-ROM.

Duan, J., M. Bevis, P. Fang, Y. Bock, S. Chiswell, S. Businger, C. Rocken, F. Solheim, T. van Hove, R. Ware, and others. 1996. GPS meteorology: direct estimation of the absolute value of precipitable water. Journal of Applied Meteorology 35:830-838.

Environmental Protection Agency. 1987. On-site meteorological program guidance for regulatory modeling applications. EPA-450/4-87-013. Environmental Protection Agency, Office of Air Quality Planning and Standards, Research Triangle Park, North Carolina.

Finklin, A. I., and W. C. Fischer. 1990. Weather station handbook –an interagency guide for wildland managers. NFES No. 2140. National Wildfire Coordinating Group, Boise, Idaho.

Gibson, W. P., C. Daly, T. Kittel, D. Nychka, C. Johns, N. Rosenbloom, A. McNab, and G. Taylor. 2002. Development of a 103-year high-resolution climate data set for the conterminous United States. Thirteenth AMS Conf. on Applied Climatology. Portland, Oregon, American Meteorological Society, Boston, MA, May 2002:181-183.

Giese, G. S. and D. G. Aubrey. 1987. Bluff erosion on outer Cape Cod. Coastal Sediments '87 Proceedings **ASCE vol. II**:1871-1876.

Godfrey, P. J., K. Galluzzo, N. Price, J. Portnoy, M. Reynolds, and D. Vana-Miller. 1999. Water Resources Management Plan, Cape Cod National Seashore, Massachusetts. NPD-160. Cape Cod National Seashore.

Groisman P. Ya., R. W. Knight, and T. R. Karl. 2000. Heavy precipitation and high streamflow in the contiguous United States: trends in the 20th Century. Bulletin of the American Meteorological Society **82**:219-246.

Hinga, K. R., A. A. Keller, and C. A. Oviatt. 1991. Atmospheric deposition and nitrogen inputs into coastal waters. Ambio **20**:256-260.

Hughes P. Y., E. H. Mason, T. R. Karl, and W. A. Brower. 1992. United States Historical Climatology Network daily temperature and precipitation data. Environmental Sciences Division Publication 3778, Carbon Dioxide Information and Analysis Center, Oak Ridge National Laboratory, Oak Ridge, Tennessee.

I&M. 2006. I&M Inventories home page. http://science.nature.nps.gov/im/inventory/index.cfm.

Jacobson, M. C., R. J. Charlson, H. Rodhe, and G. H. Orians. 2000. Earth System Science: From Biogeochemical Cycles to Global Change. Academic Press, San Diego.

Jaworski, N. A., R. W. Howarth, and L. J. Helting. 1997. Atmospheric deposition of nitrous oxides onto the landscape contributes to coastal eutrophication in the northeastern United States. Environmental Science and Technology **31**:1995-2004.

Karl, T. R., P. Ya. Groisman, R. W. Knight, and R. R. Heim, Jr. 1993. Recent variations of snow cover and snowfall in North America and their relation to precipitation and temperature variations. Journal of Climate **6**:1327-1344.

Karl, T. R., V. E. Derr, D. R. Easterling, C. K. Folland, D. J. Hoffman, S. Levitus, N. Nicholls, D. E. Parker, and G. W. Withee. 1996a. Critical issues for long-term climate monitoring. Pages 55-92 *in* T. R. Karl, editor. Long Term Climate Monitoring by the Global Climate Observing System, Kluwer Publishing.

Karl, T. R., R.W. Knight, D.R. Easterling, and R.G. Quayle, 1996b. Trends in U.S. climate during the twentieth century. Consequences **1**:2-12.

Karl, T. R., and R. W. Knight. 1998. Secular trends in precipitation amount, frequency, and intensity in the United States. Bulletin of the American Meteorological Society **79**:231-241.

Kidder, S. Q., and T. H. Vonder Haar. 1995. Satellite Meteorology: An Introduction. Academic Press, San Diego.

LeBlanc, D. R., J. H. Guswa, M. H. Frimpter, and C. J. Londquist. 1985. Ground water resources of Cape Cod, Massachusetts. Hydrological Investigations Atlas HA-692. U.S. Geological Survey, Boston, Massachusetts.

Lugo, A. E. 2000. Effects and outcomes of hurricanes in a climate change scenario. The Science of the Total Environment **262**:243-252.

Lugo, A. E., and F. N. Scatena. 1996. Background and catastrophic tree mortality in tropical moist, wet, and rain forests. Biotropica **28**:585-599.

Lyons, S. W. 2004. U.S. tropical cyclone landfall variability: 1950-2002. Weather and Forecasting **19**:473-480.

National Assessment Synthesis Team. 2001. Climate Change Impacts on the United States: The Potential Consequences of Climate Variability and Change, Report for the U.S. Global Change Research Program. Cambridge University Press, Cambridge, UK.

National Research Council. 2001. A Climate Services Vision: First Steps Toward the Future. National Academies Press, Washington, D.C.

National Wildfire Coordinating Group. 2004. National fire danger rating system weather station standards. Report PMS 426.3. National Wildfire Coordinating Group, Boise, Idaho.

Neilson, R. P. 1987. Biotic regionalization and climatic controls in western North America. Vegetatio **70**:135-147.

Nordstrom, K. F. 1992. Estuarine Beaches. Elsevier.

Nordstrom, K. F. 2000. Beaches and dunes of developed coasts. Cambridge University Press, Cambridge, UK.

Oakley, K. L., L. P. Thomas, and S. G. Fancy. 2003. Guidelines for long-term monitoring protocols. Wildlife Society Bulletin **31**:1000-1003.

Portnoy, J. W., M. G. Winkler, P. R. Sanford, and C. N. Farris. 2001. Kettle pond atlas for Cape Cod National Seashore: paleoecology and modern water chemistry. Technical Report. Cape Cod National Seashore.

Roman, C. T., J. A. Peck, J. R. Allen, J. W. King, and P. G. Appleby. 1997. Accretion of a New England (USA) salt marsh in response to inlet migration, storms, and sea level rise. Estuarine, Coastal and Shelf Science **45**:717-727.

Schlesinger, W. H. 1997. Biogeochemistry: An Analysis of Global Change. Academic Press, San Diego.

Shaver, G. R., J. Canadell, F. S. Chapin III, J. Gurevitch, J. Harte, G. Henry, P. Ineson, S. Jonasson, J. Melillo, L. Pitelka, and others. 2000. Global warming and terrestrial ecosystems: a conceptual framework for analysis. BioScience **50**:871-882.

Smith, E. 1999. Atlantic and East Coast hurricanes 1900-98: a frequency and intensity study for the twenty-first century. Bulletin of the American Meteorological Society **80**:2717-2720.

Stevens, S., B. Milstead, M. Albert, and G. Entsminger. 2005. Northeast Coastal and Barrier Network Vital Signs Monitoring Plan. Technical Report NPS/NER/NRTR--2005/025. National Park Service. Boston, Massachusetts.

Tanner, B. D. 1990. Automated weather stations. Remote Sensing Reviews **5**:73-98.

World Meteorological Organization. 1983. Guide to meteorological instruments and methods of observation, No. 8, 5th edition, World Meteorological Organization, Geneva Switzerland.

World Meteorological Organization. 2005. Organization and planning of intercomparisons of rainfall intensity gauges. World Meteorological Organization, Geneva Switzerland.

Yuan, L. L., R. A. Anthes, R. H. Ware, C. Rocken, W. D. Bonner, M. G. Bevis, and S. Businger. 1993. Sensing climate change using the global positioning system. Journal of Geophysical Research **98**:14,925-14,937.

Zeigler, J. M., C. R. Hayes, and S. D. Tuttle. 1959. Beach changes during storms on outer Cape Cod, Massachusetts. Journal of Geology **3**:318-336.

Appendix A. Glossary.

Climate—Complete and entire ensemble of statistical descriptors of temporal and spatial properties comprising the behavior of the atmosphere. These descriptors include means, variances, frequency distributions, autocorrelations, spatial correlations and other patterns of association, temporal lags, and element-to-element relationships. The descriptors have a physical basis in flows and reservoirs of energy and mass. Climate and weather phenomena shade gradually into each other and are ultimately inseparable.

Climate Element—(same as Weather Element) Attribute or property of the state of the atmosphere that is measured, estimated, or derived. Examples of climate elements include temperature, wind speed, wind direction, precipitation amount, precipitation type, relative humidity, dewpoint, solar radiation, snow depth, soil temperature at a given depth, etc. A derived element is a function of other elements (like degree days or number of days with rain) and is not measured directly with a sensor. The terms "parameter" or "variable" are not used to describe elements.

Climate Network—Group of climate stations having a common purpose; the group is often owned and maintained by a single organization.

Climate Station—Station where data are collected to track atmospheric conditions over the long-term. Often, this station operates to additional standards to verify long-term consistency. For these stations, the detailed circumstances surrounding a set of measurements (siting and exposure, instrument changes, etc.) are important.

Data—Measurements specifying the state of the physical environment. Does not include metadata.

Data Inventory—Information about overall data properties for each station within a weather or climate network. A data inventory may include start/stop dates, percentages of available data, breakdowns by climate element, counts of actual data values, counts or fractions of data types, etc. These properties must be determined by actually reading the data and thus require the data to be available, accessible, and in a readable format.

NPS I&M Network—A set of NPS park units grouped by a common theme, typically by natural resource and/or geographic region.

Metadata—Information necessary to interpret environmental data properly, organized as a history or series of snapshots—data about data. Examples include details of measurement processes, station circumstances and exposures, assumptions about the site, network purpose and background, types of observations and sensors, pre-treatment of data, access information, maintenance history and protocols, observational methods, archive locations, owner, and station start/end period.

Quality Assurance—Planned and systematic set of activities to provide adequate confidence that products and services are resulting in credible and correct information. Includes quality control.

Quality Control—Evaluation, assessment, and improvement of imperfect data by utilizing other imperfect data.

Station Inventory—Information about a set of stations obtained from metadata that accompany the network or networks. A station inventory can be compiled from direct and indirect reports prepared by others.

Weather—Instantaneous state of the atmosphere at any given time, mainly with respect to its effects on biological activities. As distinguished from climate, weather consists of the short-term (minutes to days) variations in the atmosphere. Popularly, weather is thought of in terms of temperature, precipitation, humidity, wind, sky condition, visibility, and cloud conditions.

Weather Element (same as Climate Element)—Attribute or property of the state of the atmosphere that is measured, estimated, or derived. Examples of weather elements include temperature, wind speed, wind direction, precipitation amount, precipitation type, relative humidity, dewpoint, solar radiation, snow depth, soil temperature at a given depth, etc. A derived weather element is a function of other elements (like degree days or number of days with rain) and is not measured directly. The terms "parameter" and "variable" are not used to describe weather elements.

Weather Network—Group of weather stations usually owned and maintained by a particular organization and usually for a specific purpose.

Weather Station—Station where collected data are intended for near-real-time use with less need for reference to long-term conditions. In many cases, the detailed circumstances of a set of measurements (siting and exposure, instrument changes, etc.) from weather stations are not as important as for climate stations.

Appendix B. Climate-monitoring principles.

Since the late 1990s, frequent references have been made to a set of climate-monitoring principles enunciated in 1996 by Tom Karl, director of the NOAA NCDC in Asheville, North Carolina. These monitoring principles also have been referred to informally as the "Ten Commandments of Climate Monitoring." Both versions are given here. In addition, these principles have been adopted by the Global Climate Observing System (GCOS 2004).

(Compiled by Kelly Redmond, Western Regional Climate Center, Desert Research Institute, August 2000.)

B.1. Full Version (Karl et al. 1996)

A. Effects on climate records of instrument changes, observing practices, observation locations, sampling rates, etc., must be known before such changes are implemented. This can be ascertained through a period where overlapping measurements from old and new observing systems are collected or sometimes by comparing the old and new observing systems with a reference standard. Site stability for in situ measurements, both in terms of physical location and changes in the nearby environment, also should be a key criterion in site selection. Thus, many synoptic network stations, which are primarily used in weather forecasting but also provide valuable climate data, and dedicated climate stations intended to be operational for extended periods must be subject to this policy.

B. Processing algorithms and changes in these algorithms must be well documented. Documentation should be carried with the data throughout the data-archiving process.

C. Knowledge of instrument, station, and/or platform history is essential for interpreting and using the data. Changes in instrument sampling time, local environmental conditions for in situ measurements, and other factors pertinent to interpreting the observations and measurements should be recorded as a mandatory part in the observing routine and be archived with the original data.

D. In situ and other observations with a long, uninterrupted record should be maintained. Every effort should be applied to protect the data sets that have provided long-term, homogeneous observations. "Long-term" for space-based measurements is measured in decades, but for more conventional measurements, "long-term" may be a century or more. Each element in the observational system should develop a list of prioritized sites or observations based on their contribution to long-term climate monitoring.

E. Calibration, validation, and maintenance facilities are critical requirements for long-term climatic data sets. Homogeneity in the climate record must be assessed routinely, and corrective action must become part of the archived record.

F. Where feasible, some level of "low-technology" backup to "high-technology" observing systems should be developed to safeguard against unexpected operational failures.

G. Regions having insufficient data, variables and regions sensitive to change, and key measurements lacking adequate spatial and temporal resolution should be given the highest priority in designing and implementing new climate-observing systems.

H. Network designers and instrument engineers must receive long-term climate requirements at the outset of the network design process. This is particularly important because most observing systems have been designed for purposes other than long-term climate monitoring. Instruments must possess adequate accuracy with biases small enough to document climate variations and changes.

I. Much of the development of new observational capabilities and the evidence supporting the value of these observations stem from research-oriented needs or programs. A lack of stable, long-term commitment to these observations and lack of a clear transition plan from research to operations are two frequent limitations in the development of adequate, long-term monitoring capabilities. Difficulties in securing a long-term commitment must be overcome in order to improve the climate-observing system in a timely manner with minimal interruptions.

J. Data management systems that facilitate access, use, and interpretation are essential. Freedom of access, low cost, mechanisms that facilitate use (directories, catalogs, browse capabilities, availability of metadata on station histories, algorithm accessibility and documentation, etc.) and quality control should guide data management. International cooperation is critical for successful management of data used to monitor long-term climate change and variability.

B.2. Abbreviated version, "Ten Commandments of Climate Monitoring"

A. Assess the impact of new climate-observing systems or changes to existing systems before they are implemented.

   "Thou shalt properly manage network change." (assess effects of proposed changes)

B. Require a suitable period where measurement from new and old climate-observing systems will overlap.

   "Thou shalt conduct parallel testing." (compare old and replacement systems)

C. Treat calibration, validation, algorithm-change, and data-homogeneity assessments with the same care as the data.

   "Thou shalt collect metadata." (fully document system and operating procedures)

D. Verify capability for routinely assessing the quality and homogeneity of the data including high-resolution data for extreme events.

"Thou shalt assure data quality and continuity." (assess as part of routine operating procedures)

E. Integrate assessments like those conducted by the International Panel on Climate Change into global climate-observing priorities.

"Thou shalt anticipate the use of data." (integrated environmental assessment; component in operational plan for system)

F. Maintain long-term weather and climate stations.

"Thou shalt worship historic significance." (maintain homogeneous data sets from long–term, climate-observing systems)

G. Place high priority on increasing observations in regions lacking sufficient data and in regions sensitive to change and variability.

"Thou shalt acquire complementary data." (new sites to fill observational gaps)

H. Provide network operators, designers, and instrument engineers with long-term requirements at the outset of the design and implementation phases for new systems.

"Thou shalt specify requirements for climate observation systems." (application and usage of observational data)

I. Carefully consider the transition from research-observing system to long-term operation.

"Thou shalt have continuity of purpose." (stable long-term commitments)

J. Focus on data-management systems that facilitate access, use, and interpretation of weather data and metadata.

"Thou shalt provide access to data and metadata." (readily-available weather and climate information)

B.3. Literature Cited

Karl, T. R., V. E. Derr, D. R. Easterling, C. K. Folland, D. J. Hoffman, S. Levitus, N. Nicholls, D. E. Parker, and G. W. Withee. 1996. Critical issues for long-term climate monitoring. Pages 55-92 *in* T. R. Karl, editor. Long Term Climate Monitoring by the Global Climate Observing System, Kluwer Publishing.

Global Climate Observing System. 2004. Implementation plan for the global observing system for climate in support of the UNFCCC. GCOS-92, WMO/TD No. 1219, World Meteorological Organization, Geneva, Switzerland.

Appendix C. Factors in operating a climate network.

C.1. Climate versus Weather
- Climate measurements require *consistency through time.*

C.2. Network Purpose
- Anticipated or desired lifetime.
- Breadth of network mission (commitment by needed constituency).
- Dedicated constituency—no network survives without a dedicated constituency.

C.3. Site Identification and Selection
- Spanning gradients in climate or biomes with transects.
- Issues regarding representative spatial scale—site uniformity versus site clustering.
- Alignment with and contribution to network mission.
- Exposure—ability to measure representative quantities.
- Logistics—ability to service station (Always or only in favorable weather?).
- Site redundancy (positive for quality control, negative for extra resources).
- Power—is AC needed?
- Site security—is protection from vandalism needed?
- Permitting often a major impediment and usually underestimated.

C.4. Station Hardware
- Survival—weather is the main cause of lost weather/climate data.
- Robustness of sensors—ability to measure and record in any condition.
- Quality—distrusted records are worthless and a waste of time and money.
  - High quality—will cost up front but pays off later.
  - Low quality—may provide a lower start-up cost but will cost more later (low cost can be expensive).
- Redundancy—backup if sensors malfunction.
- Ice and snow—measurements are much more difficult than rain measurements.
- Severe environments (expense is about two–three times greater than for stations in more benign settings).

C.5. Communications
- Reliability—live data have a much larger constituency.
- One-way or two-way.
  - Retrieval of missed transmissions.
  - Ability to reprogram data logger remotely.
  - Remote troubleshooting abilities.
  - Continuing versus one-time costs.
- Back-up procedures to prevent data loss during communication outages.
- Live communications increase problems but also increase value.

C.6. Maintenance
- Main reason why networks fail (and most networks do eventually fail!).

- <u>Key</u> issue with nearly every network.
- Who will perform maintenance?
- Degree of commitment and motivation to contribute.
- Periodic? On-demand as needed? Preventive?
- Equipment change-out schedules and upgrades for sensors and software.
- Automated stations require <u>skilled</u> and <u>experienced</u> labor.
- Calibration—sensors often drift (climate).
- Site maintenance essential (constant vegetation, surface conditions, nearby influences).
- Typical automated station will cost about $2K per year to maintain.
- Documentation—photos, notes, visits, changes, essential for posterity.
- Planning for equipment life cycle and technological advances.

C.7. Maintaining Programmatic Continuity and Corporate Knowledge
- Long-term vision and commitment needed.
- Institutionalizing versus personalizing—developing appropriate dependencies.

C.8. Data Flow
- Centralized ingest?
- Centralized access to data and data products?
- Local version available?
- Contract out work or do it yourself?
- Quality control of data.
- Archival.
- Metadata—historic information, not a snapshot. Every station should collect metadata.
- Post-collection processing, multiple data-ingestion paths.

C.9. Products
- Most basic product consists of the data values.
- Summaries.
- Write own applications or leverage existing mechanisms?

C.10. Funding
- Prototype approaches as proof of concept.
- Linking and leveraging essential.
- Constituencies—every network <u>needs</u> a constituency.
- Bridging to practical and operational communities? Live data needed.
- Bridging to counterpart research efforts and initiatives—funding source.
- Creativity, resourcefulness, and persistence usually are essential to success.

C.11. Final Comments
- Deployment is by far the easiest part in operating a network.
- Maintenance is the main issue.
- Best analogy: Operating a network is like raising a child; it requires constant attention.

Source: Western Regional Climate Center (WRCC)

Appendix D. General design considerations for weather/ climate-monitoring programs.

The process for designing a climate-monitoring program benefits from anticipating design and protocol issues discussed here. Much of this material is been excerpted from a report addressing the Channel Islands National Park (Redmond and McCurdy 2005), where an example is found illustrating how these factors can be applied to a specific setting. Many national park units possess some climate or meteorology feature that sets them apart from more familiar or "standard" settings.

D.1. Introduction

There are several criteria that must be used in deciding to deploy new stations and where these new stations should be sited.
- Where are existing stations located?
- Where have data been gathered in the past (discontinued locations)?
- Where would a new station fill a knowledge gap about basic, long-term climatic averages for an area of interest?
- Where would a new station fill a knowledge gap about how climate behaves over time?
- As a special case for behavior over time, what locations might be expected to show a more sensitive response to climate change?
- How do answers to the preceding questions depend on the climate element? Are answers the same for precipitation, temperature, wind, snowfall, humidity, etc.?
- What role should manual measurements play? How should manual measurements interface with automated measurements?
- Are there special technical or management issues, either present or anticipated in the next 5–15 years, requiring added climate information?
- What unique information is provided in addition to information from existing sites? "Redundancy is bad."
- What nearby information is available to estimate missing observations because observing systems always experience gaps and lose data? "Redundancy is good."
- How would logistics and maintenance affect these decisions?

In relation to the preceding questions, there are several topics that should be considered. The following topics are not listed in a particular order.

D.1.1. Network Purpose

Humans seem to have an almost reflexive need to measure temperature and precipitation, along with other climate elements. These reasons span a broad range from utilitarian to curiosity-driven. Although there are well-known recurrent patterns of need and data use, new uses are always appearing. The number of uses ranges in the thousands. Attempts have been made to categorize such uses (see NRC, 1998; NRC, 2001). Because climate measurements are accumulated over a long time, they should be treated as multi-purpose and should be undertaken in a manner that serves the widest possible applications. Some applications remain constant, while others rise and fall in importance. An insistent issue today may subside, while the next pressing issue of tomorrow barely may be anticipated. The notion that humans might affect the climate of the entire Earth was nearly unimaginable when the national USDA (later NOAA) cooperative weather network began in the late 1800s. Abundant experience has shown, however, that there always will be a demand for a history record of climate measurements and their properties. Experience also shows that there is an expectation that climate measurements will be taken and made available to the general public.

An exhaustive list of uses for data would fill many pages and still be incomplete. In broad terms, however, there are needs to document environmental conditions that disrupt or otherwise affect park operations (e.g., storms and droughts). Design and construction standards are determined by climatological event frequencies that exceed certain thresholds. Climate is a determinant that sometimes attracts and sometimes discourages visitors. Climate may play a large part in the park experience (e.g., Death Valley and heat are nearly synonymous). Some park units are large enough to encompass spatial or elevation diversity in climate, and the sequence of events can vary considerably inside or close to park boundaries. That is, temporal trends and statistics may not be the same everywhere, and this spatial structure should be sampled. The granularity of this structure depends on the presence of topography or large climate gradients or both, such as that found along the U.S. West Coast in summer with the rapid transition from the marine layer to the hot interior.

Plant and animal communities and entire ecosystems react to every nuance in the physical environment. No aspect of weather and climate goes undetected in the natural world. Wilson (1998) proposed "an informal rule of biological evolution" that applies here: "If an organic sensor can be imagined that is capable of detecting any particular environmental signal, a species exists somewhere that possesses this sensor." Every weather and climate event, whether dull or extraordinary to humans, matters to some organism. Dramatic events and creeping incremental change both have consequences to living systems. Extreme events or disturbances can "reset the clock" or "shake up the system" and lead to reverberations that last for years to centuries or longer. Slow change can carry complex nonlinear systems (e.g., any living assemblage) into states where chaotic transitions and new behavior occur. These changes are seldom predictable, typically are observed after the fact, and understood only in retrospect. Climate changes may not be exciting, but as a well-known atmospheric scientist, Mike Wallace, from the University of Washington once noted, "subtle does not mean unimportant".

Thus, individuals who observe the climate should be able to record observations accurately and depict both rapid and slow changes. In particular, an array of artificial influences easily can confound detection of slow changes. The record as provided can contain both real climate variability (that took place in the atmosphere) and fake climate variability (that arose directly from the way atmospheric changes were observed and recorded). As an example, trees growing near a climate station with an excellent anemometer will make it appear that the wind gradually slowed down over many years. Great care must be taken to protect against sources of fake climate variability on the longer-time scales of years to decades. Processes leading to the observed climate are not stationary; rather these processes draw from probability distributions that vary with time. For this reason, climatic time series do not exhibit statistical stationarity. The implications are manifold. There are no true climatic "normals" to which climate inevitably must return. Rather, there are broad ranges of climatic conditions. Climate does not demonstrate exact repetition but instead continual fluctuation and sometimes approximate repetition. In addition, there is always new behavior waiting to occur. Consequently, the business of climate monitoring is never finished, and there is no point where we can state confidently that "enough" is known.

D.1.2. Robustness

The most frequent cause for loss of weather data is the weather itself, the very thing we wish to record. The design of climate and weather observing programs should consider the meteorological equivalent of "peaking power" employed by utilities. Because environmental disturbances have significant effects on ecologic systems, sensors, data loggers, and communications networks should be able to function during the most severe conditions that realistically can be anticipated over the next 50–100 years. Systems designed in this manner are less likely to fail under more ordinary conditions, as well as more likely to transmit continuous, quality data for both tranquil and active periods.

D.1.3. Weather versus Climate

For "weather" measurements, pertaining to what is approximately happening here and now, small moves and changes in exposure are not as critical. For "climate" measurements, where values from different points in time are compared, siting and exposure are critical factors, and it is vitally important that the observing circumstances remain essentially unchanged over the duration of the station record.

Station moves can affect different elements to differing degrees. Even small moves of several meters, especially vertically, can affect temperature records. Hills and knolls act differently from the bottoms of small swales, pockets, or drainage channels (Geiger et al. 2003; Whiteman 2000). Precipitation is probably less subject to change with moves of 50–100 m than other elements (that is, precipitation has less intrinsic variation in small spaces) except if wind flow over the gauge is affected.

D.1.4. Physical Setting

Siting and exposure, and their continuity and consistency through time, significantly influence the climate records produced by a station. These two terms have overlapping connotations. We use the term "siting" in a more general sense, reserving the term "exposure" generally for the particular circumstances affecting the ability of an instrument to record measurements that are representative of the desired spatial or temporal scale.

D.1.5. Measurement Intervals

Climatic processes occur continuously in time, but our measurement systems usually record in discrete chunks of time: for example, seconds, hours, or days. These measurements often are referred to as "systematic" measurements. Interval averages may hide active or interesting periods of highly intense activity. Alternatively, some systems record "events" when a certain threshold of activity is exceeded (examples: another millimeter of precipitation has fallen, another kilometer of wind has moved past, the temperature has changed by a degree, a gust higher than 9.9 m/s has been measured). When this occurs, measurements from all sensors are reported. These measurements are known as "breakpoint" data. In relatively unchanging conditions (long calm periods or rainless weeks, for example), event recorders should send a signal that they are still "alive and well." If systematic recorders are programmed to note and periodically report the highest, lowest, and mean value within each time interval, the likelihood is reduced that interesting behavior will be glossed over or lost. With the capacity of modern data loggers, it is recommended to record and report extremes within the basic time increment (e.g., hourly or 10 minutes). This approach also assists quality-control procedures.

There is usually a trade-off between data volume and time increment, and most automated systems now are set to record approximately hourly. A number of field stations maintained by WRCC are programmed to record in 5- or 10-minute increments, which readily serve to construct an hourly value. However, this approach produces 6–12 times as much data as hourly data. These systems typically do not record details of events at sub-interval time scales, but they easily can record peak values, or counts of threshold exceedance, within the time intervals.

Thus, for each time interval at an automated station, we recommend that several kinds of information—mean or sum, extreme maximum and minimum, and sometimes standard deviation—be recorded. These measurements are useful for quality control and other purposes. Modern data loggers and office computers have quite high capacity. Diagnostic information indicating the state of solar chargers or battery voltages and their extremes is of great value. This topic will be discussed in greater detail in a succeeding section.

Automation also has made possible adaptive or intelligent monitoring techniques where systems vary the recording rate based on detection of the behavior of interest by the software. Sub-interval behavior of interest can be masked on occasion (e.g., a 5-minute extreme downpour with high-erosive capability hidden by an innocuous hourly total). Most users prefer measurements that are systematic in time because they are much easier to summarize and manipulate.

For breakpoint data produced by event reporters, there also is a need to send periodically a signal that the station is still functioning, even though there is nothing more to report. "No report" does not necessarily mean "no data," and it is important to distinguish between the actual observation that was recorded and the content of that observation (e.g., an observation of "0.00" is not the same as "no observation").

D.1.6. Mixed Time Scales

There are times when we may wish to combine information from radically different scales. For example, over the past 100 years we may want to know how the frequency of 5-minute precipitation peaks has varied or how the frequency of peak 1-second wind gusts have varied. We may also want to know over this time if nearby vegetation gradually has grown up to increasingly block the wind or to slowly improve precipitation catch. Answers to these questions require knowledge over a wide range of time scales.

D.1.7. Elements

For manual measurements, the typical elements recorded included temperature extremes, precipitation, and snowfall/snow depth. Automated measurements typically include temperature, precipitation, humidity, wind speed and direction, and solar radiation. An exception to this exists in very windy locations where precipitation is difficult to measure accurately. Automated measurements of snow are improving, but manual measurements are still preferable, as long as shielding is present. Automated measurement of frozen precipitation presents numerous challenges that have not been resolved fully, and the best gauges are quite expensive ($3–8K). Soil temperatures also are included sometimes. Soil moisture is extremely useful, but measurements are not made at many sites. In addition, care must be taken in the installation and maintenance of instruments used in measuring soil moisture. Soil properties vary tremendously in short distances as well, and it is often very difficult ("impossible") to accurately document these variations (without digging up all the soil!). In cooler climates, ultrasonic sensors that detect snow depth are becoming commonplace.

D.1.8. Wind Standards

Wind varies the most in the shortest distance, since it always decreases to zero near the ground and increases rapidly (approximately logarithmically) with height near the ground. Changes in anemometer height obviously will affect distribution of wind speed as will changes in vegetation, obstructions such as buildings, etc. A site that has a 3-m (10-ft) mast clearly will be less windy than a site that has a 6-m (20-ft) or 10-m (33-ft) mast. Historically, many U.S. airports (FAA and NWS) and most current RAWS sites have used a standard 6-m (20-ft) mast for wind measurements. Some NPS RAWS sites utilize shorter masts. Over the last decade, as Automated Surface Observing Systems (ASOSs, mostly NWS) and Automated Weather Observing Systems (AWOSs, mostly FAA) have been deployed at most airports, wind masts have been raised to 8 or 10 m (26 or 33 ft), depending on airplane clearance. The World Meteorological Organization recommends 10 m as the height for wind measurements (WMO 1983; 2005), and more groups are migrating slowly to this standard. The American Association of State Climatologists (AASC 1985) have recommended that wind be measured at 3 m, a standard geared more for agricultural applications than for general purpose uses where higher levels usually are preferred. Different anemometers have different starting thresholds; therefore, areas that frequently experience very light winds may not produce wind measurements thus affecting long-term mean estimates of wind speed. For both sustained winds (averages over a short interval of 2–60 minutes) and especially for gusts, the duration of the sampling interval makes considerable difference. For the same wind history, 1–second gusts are higher than gusts averaging 3 seconds, which in turn are greater than 5-second averages, so that the same sequence would be described with different numbers (all three systems and more are in use). Changes in the averaging procedure, or in height or exposure, can lead to "false" or "fake" climate change with no change in actual climate. Changes in any of these should be noted in the metadata.

D.1.9. Wind Nomenclature

Wind is a vector quantity having a direction and a speed. Directions can be two- or three-dimensional; they will be three-dimensional if the vertical component is important. In all common uses, winds always are denoted by the direction they blow *from* (north wind or southerly breeze). This convention exists because wind often brings weather, and thus our attention is focused upstream. However, this approach contrasts with the way ocean currents are viewed. Ocean currents usually are denoted by the direction they are moving *towards* (eastward current moves from west to east). In specialized applications (such as in atmospheric modeling), wind velocity vectors point in the direction that the wind is blowing. Thus, a southwesterly wind (from the southwest) has both northward and eastward (to the north and to the east) components. Except near mountains, wind cannot blow up or down near the ground, so the vertical component of wind often is approximated as zero, and the horizontal component is emphasized.

D.1.10. Frozen Precipitation

Frozen precipitation is more difficult to measure than liquid precipitation, especially with automated techniques. Goodison et al. (1998), Sevruk and Harmon (1984), and Yang et al. (1998, 2001) provide many of the reasons to explain this. The importance of frozen precipitation varies greatly from one setting to another. This subject was discussed in greater detail in a related inventory and monitoring report for the Alaska park units (Redmond et al. 2005).

In climates that receive frozen precipitation, a decision must be made whether or not to try to record such events accurately. This usually means that the precipitation must be turned into liquid either by falling into an antifreeze fluid solution that is then weighed or by heating the precipitation enough to melt and fall through a measuring mechanism such as a nearly-balanced tipping bucket. Accurate measurements from the first approach require expensive gauges; tipping buckets can achieve this resolution readily but are more apt to lose some or all precipitation. Improvements have been made to the heating mechanism on the NWS tipping-bucket gauge used for the ASOS to correct its numerous deficiencies making it less problematic; however, this gauge is not inexpensive. A heat supply needed to melt frozen precipitation usually requires more energy than renewable energy (solar panels or wind recharging) can provide thus AC power is needed. The availability of AC power is severely limited in many cold or remote U. S. settings. Furthermore, periods of frozen precipitation or rime often provide less-than-optimal recharging conditions with heavy clouds, short days, low-solar-elevation angles and more horizon blocking, and cold temperatures causing additional drain on the battery.

D.1.11. Save or Lose

A second consideration with precipitation is determining if the measurement should be saved (as in weighing systems) or lost (as in tipping-bucket systems). With tipping buckets, after the water has passed through the tipping mechanism, it usually just drops to the ground. Thus, there is no checksum to ensure that the sum of all the tips adds up to what has been saved in a reservoir at some location. By contrast, the weighing gauges continually accumulate until the reservoir is emptied, the reported value is the total reservoir content (for example, the height of the liquid column in a tube), and the incremental precipitation is the difference in depth between two known times. These weighing gauges do not always have the same fine resolution. Some gauges only record to the nearest centimeter, which is usually acceptable for hydrology but not necessarily for other needs. (For reference, a millimeter of precipitation can get a person in street clothes quite wet.) This is how the NRCS/USDA SNOTEL system works in climates that measure up to 3000 cm of snow in a winter. (See http://www.wcc.nrcs.usda.gov/publications for publications or http://www.wcc.nrcs.usda.gov/factpub/aib536.html for a specific description.) No precipitation is lost this way. A thin layer of oil is used to suppress evaporation, and anti-freeze ensures that frozen precipitation melts. When initially recharged, the sum of the oil and starting antifreeze solution is treated as the zero point. The anti-freeze usually is not sufficiently environmentally friendly to discharge to the ground and thus must be hauled into the area and then back out. Other weighing gauges are capable of measuring to the 0.25-mm (0.01-in.) resolution but do not have as much capacity and must be emptied more often. Day/night and storm-related thermal expansion and contraction and sometimes wind shaking can cause fluid pressure from accumulated totals to go up and down in SNOTEL gauges by small increments (commonly 0.3-3 cm, or 0.01–0.10 ft) leading to "negative precipitation" followed by similarly non-real light precipitation when, in fact, no change took place in the amount of accumulated precipitation.

D.1.12. Time

Time should always be in local standard time (LST), and daylight savings time (DST) should never be used under any circumstances with automated equipment and timers. Using DST leads to one duplicate hour, one missing hour, and a season of displaced values, as well as needless confusion and a data-management nightmare. Absolute time, such as Greenwich Mean Time (GMT) or Coordinated Universal Time (UTC), also can be used because these formats are unambiguously translatable. Since measurements only provide information about what already *has* occurred or *is* occurring and not what *will* occur, they should always be assigned to the *ending time* of the associated interval with hour 24 marking the end of the last hour of the day. In this system, midnight always represents the end of the day, not the start. To demonstrate the importance of this differentiation, we have encountered situations where police officers seeking corroborating weather data could not recall whether the time on their crime report from a year ago was the starting midnight or the ending midnight! Station positions should be known to within a few meters, easily accomplished with GPS, so that time zones and solar angles can be determined accurately.

D.1.13. Automated versus Manual

Most of this report has addressed automated measurements. Historically, most measurements are manual and typically collected once a day. In many cases, manual measurements continue because of habit, usefulness, and desire for continuity over time. Manual measurements are extremely useful and when possible should be encouraged. However, automated measurements are becoming more common. For either, it is important to record time in a logically consistent manner.

It should not be automatically assumed that newer data and measurements are "better" than older data or that manual data are "worse" than automated data. Older or simpler manual measurements are often of very high quality even if they sometimes are not in the most convenient digital format.

There is widespread desire to use automated systems to reduce human involvement. This is admirable and understandable, but every automated weather/climate station or network requires significant human attention and maintenance. A telling example concerns the Oklahoma Mesonet (see Brock et al. 1995, and bibliography at http://www.mesonet.ou.edu), a network of about 115 high–quality, automated meteorological stations spread over Oklahoma, where about 80 percent of the annual ($2–3M) budget is nonetheless allocated to humans with only about 20 percent allocated to equipment.

D.1.14. Manual Conventions

Manual measurements typically are made once a day. Elements usually consist of maximum and minimum temperature, temperature at observation time, precipitation, snowfall, snow depth, and sometimes evaporation, wind, or other information. Since it is not actually known when extremes occurred, the only logical approach, and the nationwide convention, is to ascribe the entire measurement to the time-interval date and to enter it on the form in that way. For morning observers (for example, 8 am to 8 am), this means that the maximum temperature written for today often is from yesterday afternoon and sometimes the minimum temperature for the 24-hr period actually occurred yesterday morning. However, this is understood and expected. It is often a surprise to observers to see how many maximum temperatures do not occur in the afternoon and how many minimum temperatures do not occur in the predawn hours. This is especially true in environments that are colder, higher, northerly, cloudy, mountainous, or coastal. As long as this convention is strictly followed every day, it has been shown that truly excellent climate records can result (Redmond 1992). Manual observers should reset equipment only one time per day at the official observing time. Making more than one measurement a day is discouraged strongly; this practice results in a hybrid record that is too difficult to interpret. The only exception is for total daily snowfall. New snowfall can be measured up to four times per day with no observations closer than six hours. It is well known that more frequent measurement of snow increases the annual total because compaction is a continuous process.

Two main purposes for climate observations are to establish the long-term averages for given locations and to track variations in climate. Broadly speaking, these purposes address topics of absolute and relative climate behavior. Once absolute behavior has been "established" (a task that is never finished because long-term averages continue to vary in time)—temporal variability quickly becomes the item of most interest.

D.2. Representativeness

Having discussed important factors to consider when new sites are installed, we now turn our attention to site "representativeness." In popular usage, we often encounter the notion that a site is "representative" of another site if it receives the same annual precipitation or records the same annual temperature or if some other element-specific, long-term average has a similar value. This notion of representativeness has a certain limited validity, but there are other aspects of this idea that need to be considered.

A climate monitoring site also can be said to be representative if climate records from that site show sufficiently strong temporal correlations with a large number of locations over a sufficiently large area. If station A receives 20 cm a year and station B receives 200 cm a year, these climates obviously receive quite differing amounts of precipitation. However, if their monthly, seasonal, or annual correlations are high (for example, 0.80 or higher for a particular time scale), one site can be used as a surrogate for estimating values at the other if measurements for a particular month, season, or year are missing. That is, a wet or dry month at one station is also a wet or dry month (relative to its own mean) at the comparison station. Note that high correlations on one time scale do not imply automatically that high correlations will occur on other time scales.

Likewise, two stations having similar mean climates (for example, similar annual precipitation) might not co-vary in close synchrony (for example, coastal versus interior). This may be considered a matter of climate "affiliation" for a particular location.

Thus, the representativeness of a site can refer either to the basic climatic averages for a given duration (or time window within the annual cycle) or to the extent that the site co-varies in time with respect to all surrounding locations. One site can be representative of another in the first sense but not the second, or vice versa, or neither, or both—all combinations are possible.

If two sites are perfectly correlated then, in a sense, they are "redundant." However, redundancy has value because all sites will experience missing data especially with automated equipment in rugged environments and harsh climates where outages and other problems nearly can be guaranteed. In many cases, those outages are caused by the weather, particularly by unusual weather and the very conditions we most wish to know about. Methods for filling in those values will require proxy information from this or other nearby networks. Thus, redundancy is a virtue rather than a vice.

In general, the cooperative stations managed by the NWS have produced much longer records than automated stations like RAWS or SNOTEL stations. The RAWS stations often have problems with precipitation, especially in winter, or with missing data, so that low correlations may be data problems rather than climatic dissimilarity. The RAWS records also are relatively short, so correlations should be interpreted with care. In performing and interpreting such analyses, however, we must remember that there are physical climate reasons and observational reasons why stations within a short distance (even a few tens or hundreds of meters) may not correlate well.

D.2.1. Temporal Behavior

It is possible that high correlations will occur between station pairs during certain portions of the year (i.e., January) but low correlations may occur during other portions of the year (e.g., September or October). The relative contributions of these seasons to the annual total (for precipitation) or average (for temperature) and the correlations for each month are both factors in the correlation of an aggregated time window of longer duration that encompasses those seasons (e.g., one of the year definitions such as calendar year or water year). A complete and careful evaluation ideally would include such a correlation analysis but requires more resources and data. Note that it also is possible and frequently is observed that temperatures are highly correlated while precipitation is not or vice versa, and these relations can change according to the time of year. If two stations are well correlated for all climate elements for all portions of the year, then they can be considered redundant.

With scarce resources, the initial strategy should be to try to identify locations that do not correlate particularly well, so that each new site measures something new that cannot be guessed easily from the behavior of surrounding sites. (An important caveat here is that lack of such correlation could be a result of physical climate behavior and not a result of faults with the actual measuring process; i.e., by unrepresentative or simply poor-quality data. Unfortunately, we seldom have perfect climate data.) As additional sites are added, we usually wish for some combination of unique and redundant sites to meet what amounts to essentially orthogonal constraints: new information and more reliably-furnished information.

A common consideration is whether to observe on a ridge or in a valley, given the resources to place a single station within a particular area of a few square kilometers. Ridge and valley stations will correlate very well for temperatures when lapse conditions prevail, particularly summer daytime temperatures. In summer at night or winter at daylight, the picture will be more mixed and correlations will be lower. In winter at night when inversions are common and even the rule, correlations may be zero or even negative and perhaps even more divergent as the two sites are on opposite sides of the inversion. If we had the luxury of locating stations everywhere, we would find that ridge tops generally correlate very well with other ridge tops and similarly valleys with other valleys, but ridge tops correlate well with valleys only under certain circumstances. Beyond this, valleys and ridges having similar orientations usually will correlate better with each other than those with perpendicular orientations, depending on their orientation with respect to large-scale wind flow and solar angles.

Unfortunately, we do not have stations everywhere, so we are forced to use the few comparisons that we have and include a large dose of intelligent reasoning, using what we have observed elsewhere. In performing and interpreting such analyses, we must remember that there are physical climatic reasons and observational reasons why stations within a short distance (even a few tens or hundreds of meters) may not correlate well.

Examples of correlation analyses include those for the Channel Islands and for southwest Alaska, which can be found in Redmond and McCurdy (2005) and Redmond et al. (2005). These examples illustrate what can be learned from correlation analyses. Spatial correlations generally vary by time of year. Thus, results should be displayed in the form of annual correlation cycles—for monthly mean temperature and monthly total precipitation and perhaps other climate elements like wind or humidity—between station pairs selected for climatic setting and data availability and quality.

In general, the COOP stations managed by the NWS have produced much longer records than have automated stations like RAWS or SNOTEL stations. The RAWS stations also often have problems with precipitation, especially in winter or with missing data, so that low correlations may be data problems rather than climate dissimilarity. The RAWS records are much shorter, so correlations should be interpreted with care, but these stations are more likely to be in places of interest for remote or under-sampled regions.

D.2.2. Spatial Behavior

A number of techniques exist to interpolate from isolated point values to a spatial domain. For example, a common technique is simple inverse distance weighting. Critical to the success of the simplest of such techniques is that some other property of the spatial domain, one that is influential for the mapped element, does not vary significantly. Topography greatly influences precipitation, temperature, wind, humidity, and most other meteorological elements. Thus, this criterion clearly is not met in any region having extreme topographic diversity. In such circumstances, simple Cartesian distance may have little to do with how rapidly correlation deteriorates from one site to the next, and in fact, the correlations can decrease readily from a mountain to a valley and then increase again on the next mountain. Such structure in the fields of spatial correlation is not seen in the relatively (statistically) well-behaved flat areas like those in the eastern United States.

To account for dominating effects such as topography and inland–coastal differences that exist in certain regions, some kind of additional knowledge must be brought to bear to produce meaningful, physically plausible, and observationally based interpolations. Historically, this has proven to be an extremely difficult problem, especially to perform objective and repeatable analyses. An analysis performed for southwest Alaska (Redmond et al. 2005) concluded that the PRISM (Parameter Regression on Independent Slopes Model) maps (Daly et al. 1994; 2002; Gibson et al., 2002; Doggett et al., 2004) were probably the best available. An analysis by Simpson et al. (2005) further discussed many issues in the mapping of Alaska's climate and resulted in the same conclusion about PRISM.

D.2.3. Climate-Change Detection

Although general purpose climate stations should be situated to address all aspects of climate variability, it is desirable that they also be in locations that are more sensitive to climate change from natural or anthropogenic influences should it begin to occur. The question here is how well we know such sensitivities. The polar regions and especially the North Pole are generally regarded as being more sensitive to changes in radiative forcing of climate because of positive feedbacks. The climate-change issue is quite complex because it encompasses more than just greenhouse gasses.

Sites that are in locations or climates particularly vulnerable to climate change should be favored. How this vulnerability is determined is a considerably challenging research issue. Candidate locations or situations are those that lie on the border between two major biomes or just inside the edge of one or the other. In these cases, a slight movement of the boundary in anticipated direction (toward "warmer," for example) would be much easier to detect as the boundary moves past the site and a different set of biota begin to be established. Such a vegetative or ecologic response would be more visible and would take less time to establish as a real change than would a smaller change in the center of the distribution range of a marker or key species.

D.2.4. Element-Specific Differences

The various climate elements (temperature, precipitation, cloudiness, snowfall, humidity, wind speed and direction, solar radiation) do not vary through time in the same sequence or manner nor should they necessarily be expected to vary in this manner. The spatial patterns of variability should not be expected to be the same for all elements. These patterns also should not be expected to be similar for all months or seasons. The suitability of individual sites for measurement also varies from one element to another. A site that has a favorable exposure for temperature or wind may not have a favorable exposure for precipitation or snowfall. A site that experiences proper air movement may be situated in a topographic channel, such as a river valley or a pass, which restricts the range of wind directions and affects the distribution of speed-direction categories.

D.2.5. Logistics and Practical Factors

Even with the most advanced scientific rationale, sites in some remote or climatically challenging settings may not be suitable because of the difficulty in servicing and maintaining equipment. Contributing to these challenges are scheduling difficulties, animal behavior, snow burial, icing, snow behavior, access and logistical problems, and the weather itself. Remote and elevated sites usually require far more attention and expense than a rain-dominated, easily accessible valley location.

For climate purposes, station exposure and the local environment should be maintained in their original state (vegetation especially), so that changes seen are the result of regional climate variations and not of trees growing up, bushes crowding a site, surface albedo changing, fire clearing, etc. Repeat photography has shown many examples of slow environmental change in the vicinity of a station in rather short time frames (5–20 years), and this technique should be employed routinely and frequently at all locations. In the end, logistics, maintenance, and other practical factors almost always determine the success of weather- and climate-monitoring activities.

D.2.6. Personnel Factors

Many past experiences (almost exclusively negative) strongly support the necessity to place primary responsibility for station deployment and maintenance in the hands of seasoned, highly qualified, trained, and meticulously careful personnel, the more experienced the better. Over time, even in "benign" climates but especially where harsher conditions prevail, every conceivable problem will occur and both the usual and unusual should be anticipated: weather, animals, plants, salt, sensor and communication failure, windblown debris, corrosion, power failures, vibrations, avalanches, snow loading and creep, corruption of the data logger program, etc. An ability to anticipate and forestall such problems, a knack for innovation and improvisation, knowledge of electronics, practical and organizational skills, and presence of mind to bring the various small but vital parts, spares, tools, and diagnostic troubleshooting equipment are highly valued qualities. Especially when logistics are so expensive, a premium should be placed on using experienced personnel, since the slightest and seemingly most minor mistake can render a station useless or, even worse, uncertain. Exclusive reliance on individuals without this background can be costly and almost always will result eventually in unnecessary loss of data. Skilled labor and an apprenticeship system to develop new skilled labor will greatly reduce (but not eliminate) the types of problems that can occur in operating a climate network.

D.3. Site Selection

In addition to considerations identified previously in this appendix, various factors need to be considered in selecting sites for new or augmented instrumentation.

D.3.1. Equipment and Exposure Factors

D.3.1.1. Measurement Suite: All sites should measure temperature, humidity, wind, solar radiation, and snow depth. Precipitation measurements are more difficult but probably should be attempted with the understanding that winter measurements may be of limited or no value unless an all-weather gauge has been installed. Even if an all-weather gauge has been installed, it is desirable to have a second gauge present that operates on a different principle–for example, a fluid-based system like those used in the SNOTEL stations in tandem with a higher–resolution, tipping bucket gauge for summertime. Without heating, a tipping bucket gauge usually is of use only when temperatures are above freezing and when temperatures have not been below freezing for some time, so that accumulated ice and snow is not melting and being recorded as present precipitation. Gauge undercatch is a significant issue in snowy climates, so shielding should be considered for all gauges designed to work over the winter months. It is very important to note the presence or absence of shielding, the type of shielding, and the dates of installation or removal of the shielding.

D.3.1.2. Overall Exposure: The ideal, general all-purpose site has gentle slopes, is open to the sun and the wind, has a natural vegetative cover, avoids strong local (less than 200 m) influences, and represents a reasonable compromise among all climate elements. The best temperature sites are not the best precipitation sites, and the same is true for other elements. Steep topography in the immediate vicinity should be avoided unless settings where precipitation is affected by steep topography are being deliberately sought or a mountaintop or ridgeline is the desired location. The potential for disturbance should be considered: fire and flood risk, earth movement, wind-borne debris, volcanic deposits or lahars, vandalism, animal tampering, and general human encroachment are all factors.

D.3.1.3. Elevation: Mountain climates do not vary in time in exactly the same manner as adjoining valley climates. This concept is emphasized when temperature inversions are present to a greater degree and during precipitation when winds rise up the slopes at the same angle. There is considerable concern that mountain climates will be (or already are) changing and perhaps changing differently than lowland climates, which has direct and indirect consequences for plant and animal life in the more extreme zones. Elevations of special significance are those that are near the mean rain/snow line for winter, near the tree line, and near the mean annual freezing level (all of these may not be quite the same). Because the lapse rates in wet climates often are nearly moist-adiabatic during the main precipitation seasons, measurements at one elevation may be extrapolated to nearby elevations. In drier climates and in the winter, temperature and to a lesser extent wind will show various elevation profiles.

D.3.1.4. Transects: The concept of observing transects that span climatic gradients is sound. This is not always straightforward in topographically uneven terrain, but these transects could still be arranged by setting up station(s) along the coast; in or near passes atop the main coastal interior drainage divide; and inland at one, two, or three distances into the interior lowlands. Transects need not—and by dint of topographic constraints probably cannot—be straight lines, but the closer that a line can be approximated the better. The main point is to systematically sample the key points of a behavioral transition without deviating too radically from linearity.

D.3.1.5. Other Topographic Considerations: There are various considerations with respect to local topography. Local topography can influence wind (channeling, upslope/downslope, etc.), precipitation (orographic enhancement, downslope evaporation, catch efficiency, etc.), and temperature (frost pockets, hilltops, aspect, mixing or decoupling from the overlying atmosphere, bowls, radiative effects, etc.), to different degrees at differing scales. In general, for measurements to be areally representative, it is better to avoid these local effects to the extent that they can be identified before station deployment (once deployed, it is desirable not to move a station). The primary purpose of a climate-monitoring network should be to serve as an infrastructure in the form of a set of benchmark stations for comparing other stations. Sometimes, however, it is exactly these local phenomena that we want to capture. Living organisms, especially plants, are affected by their immediate environment, whether it is representative of a larger setting or not. Specific measurements of limited scope and duration made for these purposes then can be tied to the main benchmarks. This experience is useful also in determining the complexity needed in the benchmark monitoring process in order to capture particular phenomena at particular space and time scales.

Sites that drain (cold air) well generally are better than sites that allow cold air to pool. Slightly sloped areas (1 degree is fine) or small benches from tens to hundreds of meters above streams are often favorable locations. Furthermore, these sites often tend to be out of the path of hazards (like floods) and to have rocky outcroppings where controlling vegetation will not be a major concern. Benches or wide spots on the rise between two forks of a river system are often the only flat areas and sometimes jut out to give greater exposure to winds from more directions.

D.3.1.6. Prior History: The starting point in designing a program is to determine what kinds of observations have been collected over time, by whom, in what manner, and if these observation are continuing to the present time. It also may be of value to "re-occupy" the former site of a station that is now inactive to provide some measure of continuity or a reference point from the past. This can be of value even if continuous observations were not made during the entire intervening period.

D.3.2. Element-Specific Factors

D.3.2.1. Temperature: An open exposure with uninhibited air movement is the preferred setting. The most common measurement is made at approximately eye level, 1.5–2.0 m. In snowy locations sensors should be at least one meter higher than the deepest snowpack expected in the next 50 years or perhaps 2–3 times the depth of the average maximum annual depth. Sensors should be shielded above and below from solar radiation (bouncing off snow), from sunrise/sunset horizontal input, and from vertical rock faces. Sensors should be clamped tightly, so that they do not swivel away from level stacks of radiation plates. Nearby vegetation should be kept away from the sensors (several meters). Growing vegetation should be cut to original conditions. Small hollows and swales can cool tremendously at night, and it is best avoid these areas. Side slopes of perhaps a degree or two of angle facilitate air movement and drainage and, in effect, sample a large area during nighttime hours. The very bottom of a valley should be avoided. Temperature can change substantially from moves of only a few meters. Situations have been observed where flat and seemingly uniform conditions (like airport runways) appear to demonstrate different climate behaviors over short distances of a few tens or hundreds of meters (differences of 5–10°C). When snow is on the ground, these microclimatic differences can be stronger, and differences of 2–5°C can occur in the short distance between the thermometer and the snow surface on calm evenings.

D.3.2.2. Precipitation (liquid): Calm locations with vegetative or artificial shielding are preferred. Wind will adversely impact readings; therefore, the less the better. Wind effects on precipitation are far less for rain than for snow. Devices that "save" precipitation present advantages, but most gauges are built to dump precipitation as it falls or to empty periodically. Automated gauges give both the amount and the timing. Simple backups that record only the total precipitation since the last visit have a certain advantage (for example, storage gauges or lengths of PVC pipe perhaps with bladders on the bottom). The following question should be asked: Does the total precipitation from an automated gauge add up to the measured total in a simple bucket (evaporation is prevented with an appropriate substance such as mineral oil)? Drip from overhanging foliage and trees can augment precipitation totals.

D.3.2.3. Precipitation (frozen): Calm locations or shielding are a must. Undercatch for rain is only about 5 percent, but with winds of only 2–4 m/s, gauges may catch only 30–70 percent of the actual snow falling depending on density of the flakes. To catch 100 percent of the snow, the standard configuration for shielding is employed by the CRN (Climate Reference Network): the DFIR (Double-Fence Intercomparison Reference) shield with 2.4-m (8-ft.) vertical, wooden slatted fences in two concentric octagons with diameters of 8 m and 4 m (26 ft and 13 ft, respectively) and an inner Alter shield (flapping vanes). Numerous tests have shown this is the only way to achieve complete catch of snowfall (e.g., Yang et al. 1998, 2001). The DFIR shield is large and bulky; it is recommended that all precipitation gauges have at least Alter shields on them.

Near the coast, much snow is heavy and falls more vertically. In colder locations or storms, light flakes frequently will fly in and then out of the gauge. Clearings in forests are usually excellent sites. Snow blowing from trees that are too close can augment actual precipitation totals. Artificial shielding (vanes, etc.) placed around gauges in snowy locales always should be used if accurate totals are desired. Moving parts tend to freeze up. Capping of gauges during heavy snowfall events is a common occurrence. When the cap becomes pointed, snow falls off to the ground and is not recorded. Caps and plugs often will not fall into the tube until hours, days, or even weeks have passed, typically during an extended period of freezing temperature or above or when sunlight finally occurs. Liquid-based measurements (e.g., SNOTEL "rocket" gauges) do not have the resolution (usually 0.3 cm [0.1 in.] rather than 0.03 cm [0.01 in.]) that tipping bucket and other gauges have but are known to be reasonably accurate in very snowy climates. Light snowfall events might not be recorded until enough of them add up to the next reporting increment. More expensive gauges like Geonors can be considered and could do quite well in snowy settings; however, they need to be emptied every 40 cm (15 in.) or so (capacity of 51 cm [20 in.]) until the new 91-cm (36-in.) capacity gauge is offered for sale. Recently, the NWS has been trying out the new (and very expensive) Ott all-weather gauge. Riming can be an issue in windy foggy environments below freezing. Rime, dew, and other forms of atmospheric condensation are not real precipitation, since they are caused by the gauge.

D.3.2.4. Snow Depth: Windswept areas tend to be blown clear of snow. Conversely, certain types of vegetation can act as a snow fence and cause artificial drifts. However, some amount of vegetation in the vicinity generally can help slow down the wind. The two most common types of snow-depth gauges are the Judd Snow Depth Sensor, produced by Judd Communications, and the snow depth gauge produced by Campbell Scientific, Inc. Opinions vary on which one is better. These gauges use ultrasound and look downward in a cone about 22 degrees in diameter. The ground should be relatively clear of vegetation and maintained in a manner so that the zero point on the calibration scale does not change.

D.3.2.5. Snow Water Equivalent: This is determined by the weight of snow on fluid-filled pads about the size of a desktop set up sometimes in groups of four or in larger hexagons several meters in diameter. These pads require flat ground some distance from nearby sources of windblown snow and shielding that is "just right": not too close to the shielding to act as a kind of snow fence and not too far from the shielding so that blowing and drifting become a factor. Generally, these pads require fluids that possess antifreeze-like properties, as well as handling and replacement protocols.

D.3.2.6. Wind: Open exposures are needed for wind measurements. Small prominences or benches without blockage from certain sectors are preferred. A typical rule for trees is to site stations back 10 tree-heights from all tree obstructions. Sites in long, narrow valleys can obviously only exhibit two main wind directions. Gently rounded eminences are more favored. Any kind of topographic steering should be avoided to the extent possible. Avoiding major mountain chains or single isolated mountains or ridges is usually a favorable approach, if there is a choice. Sustained wind speed and the highest gusts (1-second) should be recorded. Averaging methodologies for both sustained winds and gusts can affect climate trends and should be recorded as metadata with all changes noted. Vegetation growth affects the vertical wind profile, and growth over a few years can lead to changes in mean wind speed even if the "real" wind does not change, so vegetation near the site (perhaps out to 50 m) should be maintained in a quasi-permanent status (same height and spatial distribution). Wind devices can rime up and freeze or spin out of balance. In severely rimed or windy climates, rugged anemometers, such as those made by Taylor, are worth considering. These anemometers are expensive but durable and can withstand substantial abuse. In exposed locations, personnel should plan for winds to be at least 50 m/s and be able to measure these wind speeds. At a minimum, anemometers should be rated to 75 m/s.

D.3.2.7. Humidity: Humidity is a relatively straightforward climate element. Close proximity to lakes or other water features can affect readings. Humidity readings typically are less accurate near 100 percent and at low humidities in cold weather.

D.3.2.8. Solar Radiation: A site with an unobstructed horizon obviously is the most desirable. This generally implies a flat plateau or summit. However, in most locations trees or mountains will obstruct the sun for part of the day.

D.3.2.9. Soil Temperature: It is desirable to measure soil temperature at locations where soil is present. If soil temperature is recorded at only a single depth, the most preferred depth is 10 cm. Other common depths include 25 cm, 50 cm, 2 cm, and 100 cm. Biological activity in the soil will be proportional to temperature with important threshold effects occurring near freezing.

D.3.2.10. Soil Moisture: Soil-moisture gauges are somewhat temperamental and require care to install. The soil should be characterized by a soil expert during installation of the gauge. The readings may require a certain level of experience to interpret correctly. If accurate, readings of soil moisture are especially useful.

D.3.2.11. Distributed Observations: It can be seen readily that compromises must be struck among the considerations described in the preceding paragraphs because some are mutually exclusive.

How large can a "site" be? Generally, the equipment footprint should be kept as small as practical with all components placed next to each other (within less than 10–20 m or so). Readings from one instrument frequently are used to aid in interpreting readings from the remaining instruments.

What is a tolerable degree of separation? Some consideration may be given to locating a precipitation gauge or snow pillow among protective vegetation, while the associated temperature, wind, and humidity readings would be collected more effectively in an open and exposed location within 20–50 m. Ideally, it is advantageous to know the wind measurement precisely at the precipitation gauge, but a compromise involving a short split, and in effect a "distributed observation," could be considered. There are no definitive rules governing this decision, but it is suggested that the site footprint be kept within approximately 50 m. There also are constraints imposed by engineering and electrical factors that affect cable lengths, signal strength, and line noise; therefore, the shorter the cable the better. Practical issues include the need to trench a channel to outlying instruments or to allow lines to lie atop the ground and associated problems with animals, humans, weathering, etc. Separating a precipitation gauge up to 100 m or so from an instrument mast may be an acceptable compromise if other factors are not limiting.

D.3.2.12. Instrument Replacement Schedules: Instruments slowly degrade, and a plan for replacing them with new, refurbished, or recalibrated instruments should be in place. After approximately five years, a systematic change-out procedure should result in replacing most sensors in a network. Certain parts, such as solar radiation sensors, are candidates for annual calibration or change-out. Anemometers tend to degrade as bearings erode or electrical contacts become uneven. Noisy bearings are an indication, and a stethoscope might aid in hearing such noises. Increased internal friction affects the threshold starting speed; once spinning, they tend to function properly. Increases in starting threshold speeds can lead to more zero-wind measurements and thus reduce the reported mean wind speed with no real change in wind properties. A field calibration kit should be developed and taken on all site visits, routine or otherwise. Rain gauges can be tested with drip testers during field visits. Protective conduit and tight water seals can prevent abrasion and moisture problems with the equipment, although seals can keep moisture in as well as out. Bulletproof casings sometimes are employed in remote settings. A supply of spare parts, at least one of each and more for less-expensive or more-delicate sensors, should be maintained to allow replacement of worn or nonfunctional instruments during field visits. In addition, this approach allows instruments to be calibrated in the relative convenience of the operational home—the larger the network, the greater the need for a parts depot.

D.3.3. Long-Term Comparability and Consistency

D.3.3.1. Consistency: The emphasis here is to hold biases constant. Every site has biases, problems, and idiosyncrasies of one sort or another. The best rule to follow is simply to try to keep biases constant through time. Since the goal is to track climate through time, keeping sensors, methodologies, and exposure constant will ensure that only true climate change is being measured. This means leaving the site in its original state or performing maintenance to keep it that way. Once a site is installed, the goal should be to never move the site even by a few meters or to allow significant changes to occur within 100 m for the next several decades.

Sites in or near rock outcroppings likely will experience less vegetative disturbance or growth through the years and will not usually retain moisture, a factor that could speed corrosion. Sites that will remain locally similar for some time are usually preferable. However, in some cases the intent of a station might be to record the local climate effects of changes within a small-scale system (for example, glacier, recently burned area, or scene of some other disturbance) that is subject to a regional climate influence. In this example, the local changes might be much larger than the regional changes.

D.3.3.2. Metadata: Since the climate of every site is affected by features in the immediate vicinity, it is vital to record this information over time and to update the record repeatedly at each service visit. Distances, angles, heights of vegetation, fine-scale topography, condition of instruments, shielding discoloration, and other factors from within a meter to several kilometers should be noted. Systematic photography should be undertaken and updated at least once every one–two years.

Photographic documentation should be taken at each site in a standard manner and repeated every two–three years. Guidelines for methodology were developed by Redmond (2004) as a result of experience with the NOAA CRN and can be found on the WRCC NPS Web pages at www.wrcc.dri.edu/nps and at ftp.wrcc.dri.edu/nps/photodocumentation.pdf.

The main purpose for climate stations is to *track climatic conditions through time*. Anything that affects the interpretation of records through time must to be noted and recorded for posterity. The important factors should be clear to a person who has never visited the site, no matter how long ago the site was installed.

In regions with significant, climatic transition zones, transects are an efficient way to span several climates and make use of available resources. Discussions on this topic at greater detail can be found in Redmond and Simeral (2004) and in Redmond et al. (2005).

D.4. Literature Cited

American Association of State Climatologists. 1985. Heights and exposure standards for sensors on automated weather stations. The State Climatologist **9**.

Brock, F. V., K. C. Crawford, R. L. Elliott, G. W. Cuperus, S. J. Stadler, H. L. Johnson and M. D. Eilts. 1995. The Oklahoma Mesonet: A technical overview. Journal of Atmospheric and Oceanic Technology **12**:5-19.

Daly, C., R. P. Neilson, and D. L. Phillips. 1994. A statistical-topographic model for mapping climatological precipitation over mountainous terrain. Journal of Applied Meteorology **33**:140-158.

Daly, C., W. P. Gibson, G. H. Taylor, G. L. Johnson, and P. Pasteris. 2002. A knowledge-based approach to the statistical mapping of climate. Climate Research **22**:99-113.

Doggett, M., C. Daly, J. Smith, W. Gibson, G. Taylor, G. Johnson, and P. Pasteris. 2004. High-resolution 1971-2000 mean monthly temperature maps for the western United States. Fourteenth AMS Conf. on Applied Climatology, 84th AMS Annual Meeting. Seattle, WA, American Meteorological Society, Boston, MA, January 2004, Paper 4.3, CD-ROM.

Geiger, R., R. H. Aron, and P. E. Todhunter. 2003. The Climate Near the Ground. 6th edition. Rowman & Littlefield Publishers, Inc., New York.

Gibson, W. P., C. Daly, T. Kittel, D. Nychka, C. Johns, N. Rosenbloom, A. McNab, and G. Taylor. 2002. Development of a 103-year high-resolution climate data set for the conterminous United States. Thirteenth AMS Conf. on Applied Climatology. Portland, OR, American Meteorological Society, Boston, MA, May 2002:181-183.

Goodison, B. E., P. Y. T. Louie, and D. Yang. 1998. WMO solid precipitation measurement intercomparison final report. WMO TD 982, World Meteorological Organization, Geneva, Switzerland.

National Research Council. 1998. Future of the National Weather Service Cooperative Weather Network. National Academies Press, Washington, D.C.

National Research Council. 2001. A Climate Services Vision: First Steps Toward the Future. National Academies Press, Washington, D.C.

Redmond, K. T. 1992. Effects of observation time on interpretation of climatic time series - A need for consistency. Eighth Annual Pacific Climate (PACLIM) Workshop. Pacific Grove, CA, March 1991:141-150.

Redmond, K. T. 2004. Photographic documentation of long-term climate stations. Available from ftp://ftp.wrcc.dri.edu/nps/photodocumentation.pdf. (accessed 15 August 2004)

Redmond, K. T. and D. B. Simeral. 2004. Climate monitoring comments: Central Alaska Network Inventory and Monitoring Program. Available from ftp://ftp.wrcc.dri.edu/nps/alaska/cakn/npscakncomments040406.pdf. (accessed 6 April 2004)

Redmond, K. T., D. B. Simeral, and G. D. McCurdy. 2005. Climate monitoring for southwest Alaska national parks: network design and site selection. Report 05-01. Western Regional Climate Center, Reno, Nevada.

Redmond, K. T., and G. D. McCurdy. 2005. Channel Islands National Park: Design considerations for weather and climate monitoring. Report 05-02. Western Regional Climate Center, Reno, Nevada.

Sevruk, B., and W. R. Hamon. 1984. International comparison of national precipitation gauges with a reference pit gauge. Instruments and Observing Methods, Report No 17, WMO/TD – 38, World Meteorological Organization, Geneva, Switzerland.

Simpson, J. J., Hufford, G. L., C. Daly, J. S. Berg, and M. D. Fleming. 2005. Comparing maps of mean monthly surface temperature and precipitation for Alaska and adjacent areas of Canada produced by two different methods. Arctic **58**:137-161.

Whiteman, C. D. 2000. Mountain Meteorology: Fundamentals and Applications. Oxford University Press, Oxford, UK.

Wilson, E. O. 1998. Consilience: The Unity of Knowledge. Knopf, New York.

World Meteorological Organization. 1983. Guide to meteorological instruments and methods of observation, No. 8, 5th edition, World Meteorological Organization, Geneva Switzerland.

World Meteorological Organization. 2005. Organization and planning of intercomparisons of rainfall intensity gauges. World Meteorological Organization, Geneva Switzerland.

Yang, D., B. E. Goodison, J. R. Metcalfe, V. S. Golubev, R. Bates, T. Pangburn, and C. Hanson. 1998. Accuracy of NWS 8" standard nonrecording precipitation gauge: results and application of WMO intercomparison. Journal of Atmospheric and Oceanic Technology **15**:54-68.

Yang, D., B. E. Goodison, J. R. Metcalfe, P. Louie, E. Elomaa, C. Hanson, V. Bolubev, T. Gunther, J. Milkovic, and M. Lapin. 2001. Compatibility evaluation of national precipitation gauge measurements. Journal of Geophysical Research **106**:1481-1491.

Appendix E. Master metadata field list.

Field Name	Field Type	Field Description
begin_date	date	Effective beginning date for a record.
begin_date_flag	char(2)	Flag describing the known accuracy of the begin date for a station.
best_elevation	float(4)	Best known elevation for a station (in feet).
clim_div_code	char(2)	Foreign key defining climate division code (primary in table: clim_div).
clim_div_key	int2	Foreign key defining climate division for a station (primary in table: clim_div.
clim_div_name	varchar(30)	English name for a climate division.
controller_info	varchar(50)	Person or organization who maintains the identifier system for a given weather or climate network.
country_key	int2	Foreign key defining country where a station resides (primary in table: none).
county_key	int2	Foreign key defining county where a station resides (primary in table: county).
county_name	varchar(31)	English name for a county.
description	text	Any description pertaining to the particular table.
end_date	date	Last effective date for a record.
end_date_flag	char(2)	Flag describing the known accuracy of station end date.
fips_country_code	char(2)	FIPS (federal information processing standards) country code.
fips_state_abbr	char(2)	FIPS state abbreviation for a station.
fips_state_code	char(2)	FIPS state code for a station.
history_flag	char(2)	Describes temporal significance of an individual record among others from the same station.
id_type_key	int2	Foreign key defining the id_type for a station (usually defined in code).
last_updated	date	Date of last update for a record.
latitude	float(8)	Latitude value.
longitude	float(8)	Longitude value.
name_type_key	int2	"3": COOP station name, "2": best station name.
name	varchar(30)	Station name as known at date of last update entry.
ncdc_state_code	char(2)	NCDC, two-character code identifying U.S. state.
network_code	char(8)	Eight-character abbreviation code identifying a network.
network_key	int2	Foreign key defining the network for a station (primary in table: network).
network_station_id	int4	Identifier for a station in the associated network, which is defined by id_type_key.
remark	varchar(254)	Additional information for a record.
src_quality_code	char(2)	Code describing the data quality for the data source.
state_key	int2	Foreign key defining the U.S. state where a station resides (primary in table: state).
state_name	varchar(30)	English name for a state.
station_alt_name	varchar(30)	Other English names for a station.
station_best_name	varchar(30)	Best, most well-known English name for a station.
time_zone	float4	Time zone where a station resides.
ucan_station_id	int4	Unique station identifier for every station in ACIS.
unit_key	int2	Integer value representing a unit of measure.

Field Name	Field Type	Field Description
updated_by	char(8)	Person who last updated a record.
var_major_id	int2	Defines major climate variable.
var_minor_id	int2	Defines data source within a var_major_id.
zipcode	char(5)	Zipcode where a latitude/longitude point resides.
nps_netcode	char(4)	Network four-character identifier.
nps_netname	varchar(128)	Displayed English name for a network.
parkcode	char(4)	Park four-character identifier.
parkname	varchar(128)	Displayed English name for a park/
im_network	char(4)	NPS I&M network where park belongs (a net code)/
station_id	varchar(16)	Station identifier.
station_id_type	varchar(16)	Type of station identifier.
network.subnetwork.id	varchar(16)	Identifier of a sub-network in associated network.
subnetwork_key	int2	Foreign key defining sub-network for a station.
subnetwork_name	varchar(30)	English name for a sub-network.
slope	integer	Terrain slope at the location.
aspect	integer	Terrain aspect at the station.
gps	char(1)	Indicator of latitude/longitude recorded via GPS (global positioning system).
site_description	text(0)	Physical description of site.
route_directions	text(0)	Driving route or site access directions.
station_photo_id	integer	Unique identifier associating a group of photos to a station. Group of photos all taken on same date.
photo_id	char(30)	Unique identifier for a photo.
photo_date	datetime	Date photograph taken.
photographer	varchar(64)	Name of photographer.
maintenance_date	datetime	Date of station maintenance visit.
contact_key	Integer	Unique identifier associating contact information to a station.
full_name	varchar(64)	Full name of contact person.
organization	varchar(64)	Organization of contact person.
contact type	varchar(32)	Type of contact person (operator, administrator, etc.)
position_title	varchar(32)	Title of contact person.
address	varchar(32)	Address for contact person.
city	varchar(32)	City for contact person.
state	varchar(2)	State for contact person.
zip_code	char(10)	Zipcode for contact person.
country	varchar(32)	Country for contact person.
email	varchar(64)	E-mail for contact person.
work_phone	varchar(16)	Work phone for contact person.
contact_notes	text(254)	Other details regarding contact person.
equipment_type	char(30)	Sensor measurement type; i.e., wind speed, air temperature, etc.
eq_manufacturer	char(30)	Manufacturer of equipment.
eq_model	char(20)	Model number of equipment.
serial_num	char(20)	Serial number of equipment.
eq_description	varchar(254)	Description of equipment.
install_date	datetime	Installation date of equipment.
remove_date	datetime	Removal date of equipment.
ref_height	integer	Sensor displacement height from surface.
sampling_interval	varchar(10)	Frequency of sensor measurement.

Appendix F. Electronic supplements.

F.1. ACIS metadata file for weather and climate stations associated with the NCBN:
http://www.wrcc.dri.edu/nps/pub/ncbn/metadata/NCBN_from_ACIS.tar.gz.

F.2. NCBN metadata files for weather and climate stations associated with the NCBN:
http://www.wrcc.dri.edu/nps/pub/ncbn/metadata/NCBN_NPS.tar.gz.

Appendix G. Descriptions of weather/climate monitoring networks.

G.1. NWS Cooperative Observer Program (COOP)

- Purpose of network:
  - o Provide observational, meteorological data required to define U.S. climate and help measure long-term climate changes.
  - o Provide observational, meteorological data in near real-time to support forecasting and warning mechanisms and other public service programs of the NWS.
- Primary management agency: NOAA (NWS).
- Data website: data are available from the NCDC (http://www.ncdc.noaa.gov), RCCs (e.g., WRCC, http://www.wrcc.dri.edu), and state climate offices.
- Measured weather/climate elements
  - o Maximum, minimum, and observation-time temperature.
  - o Precipitation, snowfall, snow depth.
  - o Pan evaporation (some stations).
- Sampling frequency: daily.
- Reporting frequency: daily or monthly (station-dependent).
- Estimated station cost: $2K with maintenance costs of $500–900/year.
- Network strengths:
  - o Decade–century records at most sites.
  - o Widespread national coverage (thousands of stations).
  - o Excellent data quality when well maintained.
  - o Relatively inexpensive; highly cost effective.
  - o Manual measurements; not automated.
- Network weaknesses:
  - o Uneven exposures; many are not well-maintained.
  - o Dependence on schedules for volunteer observers.
  - o Slow entry of data from many stations into national archives.
  - o Data subject to observational methodology; not always documented.
  - o Manual measurements; not automated and not hourly.

The COOP network has long served as the main climate observation network in the United States. Readings are usually made by volunteers using equipment supplied, installed, and maintained by the federal government. The observer in effect acts as a host for the data-gathering activities and supplies the labor; this is truly a "cooperative" effort. The SAO sites often are considered to be part of the cooperative network as well if they collect the previously mentioned types of weather/climate observations. Typical observation days are morning to morning, evening to evening, or midnight to midnight. By convention, observations are ascribed to the date the instrument was reset at the end of the observational period. For this reason, midnight observations represent the end of a day. The Historical Climate Network is a subset of the cooperative network but contains longer and more complete records.

G.2. Citizen's Weather Observer Program (CWOP)

- Purpose of network: collect observations from private citizens and make these data available for homeland security and other weather applications, providing constant feedback to the observers to maintain high data quality.
- Primary management agency: NOAA MADIS program.
- Data Website: http://www.wxqa.com.
- Measured weather/climate elements:
  - Air temperature.
  - Dewpoint temperature.
  - Precipitation.
  - Wind speed and direction.
  - Barometric Pressure.
- Sampling frequency: 15 minutes or less.
- Reporting frequency: 15 minutes.
- Estimated station cost: unknown.
- Network strengths:
  - Active partnership between public agencies and private citizens.
  - Large number of participant sites.
  - Regular communications between data providers and users, encouraging higher data quality.
- Network weaknesses:
  - Variable instrumentation platforms.
  - Metadata are sometimes limited.

The CWOP network is a public-private partnership with U.S. citizens and various agencies including NOAA, NASA (National Aeronautics and Space Administration), and various universities. There are over 4500 registered sites worldwide, with close to 3000 of these sites located in North America.

G.3. NPS Gaseous Pollutant Monitoring Program (GPMP)

- Purpose of network: measurement of ozone and related meteorological elements.
- Primary management agency: NPS.
- Data website: http://www2.nature.nps.gov/air/monitoring.
- Measured weather/climate elements:
  - Air temperature.
  - Relative humidity
  - Precipitation.
  - Wind speed and direction.
  - Solar radiation.
  - Surface wetness
- Sampling frequency: continuous.
- Reporting frequency: hourly.
- Estimated station cost: unknown.
- Network strengths:
  - Stations are located within NPS park units.

o Data quality is excellent, with high data standards.
o Provides unique measurements that are not available elsewhere.
o Records are up to 2 decades in length.
o Site maintenance is excellent.
o Thermometers are aspirated.
- Network weaknesses:
  o Not easy to download the entire data set or to ingest live data.
  o Period of record is short compared to other automated networks. Earliest sites date from 2004.
  o Station spacing and coverage: station installation is episodic, driven by opportunistic situations.

The NPS web site indicates that there are 33 sites with continuous ozone analysis run by NPS, with records from a few to about 16-17 years. Of these stations, 12 are labeled as GPMP sites and the rest are labeled as CASTNet sites. All of these have standard meteorological measurements, including a 10-m mast. Another 9 GPMP sites are located within NPS units but run by cooperating agencies. A number of other sites (1-2 dozen) ran for differing periods in the past, generally less than 5-10 years.

G.4. NOAA Ground-Based GPS Meteorology (GPS-MET)

- Purpose of network:
  o Measure atmospheric water vapor using ground-based GPS receivers.
  o Facilitate use of these data operational and in other research and applications.
  o Provides data for weather forecasting, atmospheric modeling and prediction, climate monitoring, calibrating and validation other observing systems including radiosondes and satellites, and research.
- Primary management agency: NOAA Earth System Research Laboratory.
- Data website: http://gpsmet.noaa.gov/jsp/index.jsp.
- Measurements:
  o Dual frequency carrier phase measurements every 30 seconds
- Ancillary weather/climate observations:
  o Air temperature.
  o Relative humidity.
  o Pressure.
- Reporting frequency: currently 30 min.
- Estimated station cost: $0-$10K, depending on approach. Data from dual frequency GPS receivers installed for conventional applications (e.g. high accuracy surveying) can be used without modification.
- Network strengths:
  o Frequent, high-quality measurements.
  o High reliability.
  o All-weather operability.
  o Many uses.
  o Highly leveraged.
  o Requires no calibration.

o Measurement accuracy improves with time.
- Network weakness:
  o Point measurement.
  o Provides no direct information about the vertical distribution of water vapor.

The GPS-MET network is the first network of its kind dedicated to GPS meteorology (see Duan et al. 1996). The GPS-MET network was developed in response to the need for improved moisture observations to support weather forecasting, climate monitoring, and other research activities. GPS-MET is a collaboration between NOAA and several other governmental and university organizations and institutions.

GPS meteorology utilizes the radio signals broadcast by the satellite Global Positioning System for atmospheric remote sensing. GPS meteorology applications have evolved along two paths: ground-based (Bevis et al. 1992) and space-based (Yuan et al. 1993). Both applications make the same fundamental measurement (the apparent delay in the arrival of radio signals caused by changes in the radio-refractivity of the atmosphere along the paths of the radio signals) but they do so from different perspectives.

In ground-based GPS meteorology, a GPS receiver and antenna are placed at a fixed location on the ground and the signals from all GPS satellites in view are continuously recorded. From this information, the exact position of the GPS antenna can be determined over time with high (millimeter-level) accuracy. Subsequent measurements of the antenna position are compared with the known position, and the differences can be attributed to changes in the temperature, pressure and water vapor in the atmosphere above the antenna. By making continuous measurements of temperature and pressure at the site, the total amount of water vapor in the atmosphere at this location can be estimated with high accuracy under all weather conditions. For more information on ground based GPS meteorology the reader is referred to http://gpsmet.noaa.gov.

In space-based GPS meteorology, GPS receivers and antennas are placed on satellites in Low Earth Orbit (LEO), and the signals transmitted by a GPS satellite are continuously recorded as a GPS satellite "rises" or "sets" behind the limb of the Earth. This process is called an occultation or a limb sounding. The GPS radio signals bend more as they encounter a thicker atmosphere and the bending (which causes an apparent increase in the length of the path of the radio signal) can be attributed to changes in temperature, pressure and water vapor along the path of the radio signal through the atmosphere that is nominally about 300 km long. The location of an occultation depends on the relative geometries of the GPS satellites in Mid Earth Orbit and the satellites in LEO. As a consequence, information about the vertical temperature, pressure and moisture structure of the Earth's atmosphere as a whole can be estimated with high accuracy, but not at any one particular place over time. The main difference between ground and space-based GPS meteorology is one of geometry. A space-based measurement can be thought of as a ground-based measurement turned on its side. For more information on space based GPS meteorology, the reader is referred to http://www.cosmic.ucar.edu/gpsmet/.

G.5. Portable Ozone Monitoring System (POMS)

- Purpose of network: provide seasonal, short-term (1-5 years) monitoring of near-surface atmospheric ozone levels in remote locations.
- Primary management agency: NPS.
- Data website: http://www2.nature.nps.gov/air/studies/portO3.htm.
- Measured weather/climate elements:
  - Air temperature.
  - Precipitation.
  - Relative Humidity
  - Wind speed and direction.
  - Solar radiation.
- Sampling frequency: hourly.
- Reporting frequency: hourly.
- Estimated station cost: $20K with operation and maintenance costs of up to $10K/year.
- Network strengths:
  - High-quality data.
  - Site maintenance is excellent.
- Network weaknesses:
  - No long-term sites, so not as useful for climate monitoring.
  - Sites are somewhat expensive to operate.

The POMS network of stations is owned and operated by the NPS Air Resources Division. Since the primarily role of the network is ozone monitoring, weather observations are a secondary objective.

G.6. Remote Automated Weather Station Network (RAWS)

- Purpose of network: provide near-real-time (hourly or near hourly) measurements of meteorological variables for use in fire weather forecasts and climatology. Data from RAWS also are used for natural resource management, flood forecasting, natural hazard management, and air-quality monitoring.
- Primary management agency: WRCC, National Interagency Fire Center.
- Data website: http://www.raws.dri.edu/index.html.
- Measured weather/climate elements:
  - Air temperature.
  - Precipitation.
  - Relative humidity.
  - Wind speed.
  - Wind direction.
  - Wind gust.
  - Gust direction.
  - Solar radiation.
  - Soil moisture and temperature.
- Sampling frequency: 1 or 10 minutes, element-dependent.
- Reporting frequency: generally hourly. Some stations report every 15 or 30 minutes.

- Estimated station cost: $12K with satellite telemetry ($8K without satellite telemetry); maintenance costs are around $2K/year.
- Network strengths:
  - Metadata records are usually complete.
  - Sites are located in remote areas.
  - Sites are generally well-maintained.
  - Entire period of record available on-line.
- Network weaknesses:
  - RAWS network is focused largely on fire management needs (formerly focused only on fire needs).
  - Frozen precipitation is not measured reliably.
  - Station operation is not always continuous.
  - Data transmission is completed via one-way telemetry. Data are therefore recoverable either in real-time or not at all.

The RAWS network is used by many land-management agencies, such as the BLM, NPS, Fish and Wildlife Service, Bureau of Indian Affairs, Forest Service, and other agencies. The RAWS network was one of the first automated weather station networks to be installed in the United States. Most gauges do not have heaters, so hydrologic measurements are of little value when temperatures dip below freezing or reach freezing after frozen precipitation events. There are approximately 1,100 real-time sites in this network and about 1,800 historic sites (some are decommissioned or moved). The sites can transmit data all winter but may be in deep snow in some locations. The WRCC is the archive for this network and receives station data and metadata through a special connection to the National Interagency Fire Center in Boise, Idaho.

G.7. NWS Surface Airways Observations Network (SAO)

- Purpose of network: provide near-real-time (hourly or near hourly) measurements of meteorological variables and are used both for airport operations and weather forecasting.
- Primary management agency: NOAA, FAA.
- Data website: data are available from state climate offices, RCCs (e.g., WRCC, http://www.wrcc.dri.edu), and NCDC (http://www.ncdc.noaa.gov).
- Measured weather/climate elements:
  - Air temperature.
  - Dewpoint and/or relative humidity.
  - Wind speed.
  - Wind direction.
  - Wind gust.
  - Gust direction.
  - Barometric pressure.
  - Precipitation (not at many FAA sites).
  - Sky cover.
  - Ceiling (cloud height).
  - Visibility.
- Sampling frequency: element-dependent.
- Reporting frequency: element-dependent.

- Estimated station cost: $100–$200K with maintenance costs approximately $10K/year.
- Network strengths:
  - Records generally extend over several decades.
  - Consistent maintenance and station operations.
  - Data record is reasonably complete and usually high quality.
  - Hourly or sub-hourly data.
- Network weaknesses:
  - Nearly all sites are located at airports.
  - Data quality can be related to size of airport—smaller airports tend to have poorer datasets.
  - Influences from urbanization and other land-use changes.

These stations are managed by NOAA, U. S. Navy, U. S. Air Force, and FAA. These stations are located generally at major airports and military bases. The FAA stations often do not record precipitation, or they may provide precipitation records of reduced quality. Automated stations are typically ASOSs for the NWS or AWOSs for the FAA. Some sites only report episodically with observers paid per observation.

G.8. Weather For You Network (WX4U)

- Purpose of network: allow volunteer weather enthusiasts around the U.S. to observe and share weather data.
- Data website: http://www.met.utah.edu/jhorel/html/mesonet.
- Measured weather/climate elements:
  - Air temperature.
  - Relative humidity and dewpoint temperature.
  - Precipitation.
  - Wind speed and direction.
  - Wind gust and direction.
  - Pressure.
- Sampling frequency: 10 minutes.
- Reporting frequency: 10 minutes.
- Estimated station cost: unknown.
- Network strengths:
  - Stations are located throughout the U.S.
  - Stations provide near-real-time observations
- Network weaknesses:
  - Instrumentation platforms can be variable.
  - Data are sometimes of questionable quality.

The WX4U network is a nationwide collection of weather stations run by local observers. Meteorological elements that are measured usually include temperature, precipitation, wind, and humidity.

Appendix H. Additional weather/climate stations.*

Name	Lat.	Lon.	Elev. (m)	Network	Start	End
Truro – Fire Mgmt. Office	M	M	M	M	M	M
Truro – State of MA	M	M	M	M	M	M
S. District Fire Stn	M	M	M	M	M	M
Duck Pond (Wellfleet)	M	M	M	NPS MISC	M	M
Salt Pond Visitor Ctr (Eastham)	M	M	M	NPS MISC	M	M
Sandy Hook Ranger Stn.	M	M	M	NPS MISC	M	M
Sandy Hook Residence	M	M	M	NPS MISC	M	M
Staten Island	M	M	M	NPS MISC	M	M
Jamaica Bay Ranger Stn.	M	M	M	NPS MISC	M	M
ASIS Visitor Center Rain Gauge #1	M	M	M	NPS MISC	M	M
ASIS Visitor Center Rain Gauge #2	M	M	M	NPS MISC	M	M
ASIS NADP	M	M	M	NADP	M	M
VA Chesapeake Natl. Estuarine Research Reserve	M	M	M	M	M	M

* – "M" indicates missing information. Station names are not official, but rather are derived from station descriptions as outlined in CACO (2001) and in Conner and Albert (2004).

NPS/NCBN/NRTR—2006/008, September 2006

www.ingramcontent.com/pod-product-compliance
Lightning Source LLC
Chambersburg PA
CBHW081114290526
45795CB00006B/2116